Achieving Inner Peace

COMPONENTS OF INNER PEACE

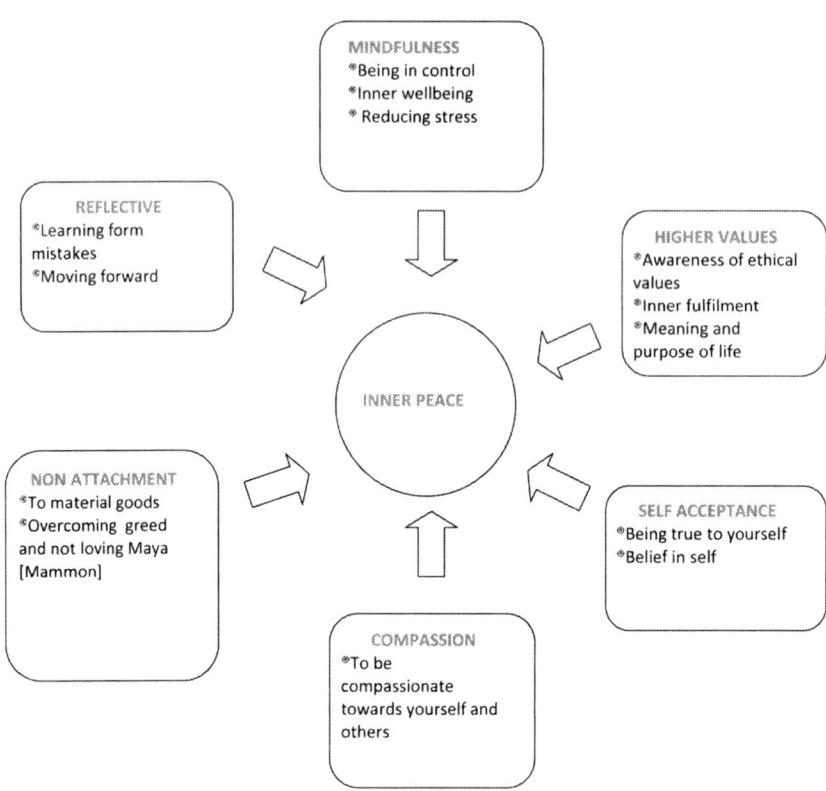

MINDFULNESS
*Being in control
*Inner wellbeing
* Reducing stress

REFLECTIVE
*Learning form
mistakes
*Moving forward

HIGHER VALUES
*Awareness of ethical
values
*Inner fulfilment
*Meaning and
purpose of life

INNER PEACE

NON ATTACHMENT
*To material goods
*Overcoming greed
and not loving Maya
[Mammon]

SELF ACCEPTANCE
*Being true to yourself
*Belief in self

COMPASSION
*To be
compassionate
towards yourself and
others

ALSO BY SOHAN SINGH

Achieving a Healthy Balanced Life!

Achieving Inner Peace

Sohan Singh, MA. BSc (Hons).
CQSW

iUniverse, Inc.
New York Bloomington Shanghai

Achieving Inner Peace

iUniverse books may be ordered through booksellers or by contacting:

iUniverse
1663 Liberty Drive
Bloomington, IN 47403
www.iuniverse.com
1-800-Authors (1-800-288-4677)

Because of the dynamic nature of the Internet, any Web addresses or links contained in this book may have changed since publication and may no longer be valid.

The views expressed in this work are solely those of the author and do not necessarily reflect the views of the publisher, and the publisher hereby disclaims any responsibility for them.

ISBN: 978-0-595-50493-0 (pbk)
ISBN: 978-0-595-61534-6 (ebk)

Printed in the United States of America

To Humanity

All mankind is one, though misgivings are many.

—*Guru Granth Sahib*

Contents

Acknowledgements

When I conceived the idea to expand on some of the themes in *Achieving a Healthy Balanced Life!* and write this book, I thought it would be a straightforward task. As in most things, experience has turned out to be different. However, a very positive outcome was that my search for 'Inner Peace' led me to talks with people, to attend lectures and read the works of authors who, I thought, knew 'the way.' Their talks and writings made me look inwards, to reflect, and to explore my own inner equilibrium. Many people have thus directly or indirectly contributed in bringing this book to fruition.

I am indebted to Rev. Diana Macnaughton for her constructive feedback, and for providing advice and help whenever needed.

I am also grateful to Ahmad Khoshnoudi for his help with the IT system, and for being 'at my service' whenever I was stuck.

I would also like to acknowledge the following for assisting me in the creation of this book:

- All my family and friends who inspired and encouraged me.

- My literary agent and editor, Dr. Charles Muller of Diadem Books, for being so positive and encouraging every time I communicate with him.

- All those who gave me gems of wisdom whenever I talked about 'Inner Peace' with them.

Thank you all.

Introduction

Life today is short on inner peace. People have their own definition of what constitutes inner peace. For some tranquillity is probably a long walk in the country far from motorways, manmade noise, getting away from it all, having time to think and feel inspired. Some might feel that peace is floating in the sea or lazing on a sunny beach. They need to be taken out of themselves and be with nature. For them peace is in the sound of the sea, the majesty of the mountains and the swooping of the bird.

For others, feeling at peace is in the mind. They believe that inner peace is about self-analysis, internal enrichment and access to their inner self. We do not have time to go in to our souls, to access our spirit. We are inundated with desires and our inner voice gets drowned. This book is about sublimating to higher desires, being captivated by higher interests and higher values.

We all want others to listen to us, to pay attention to what we have to say, but we do not want to listen to our own inner voice. We want to have a good life, though we are vague when asked what constitutes a good life. We give advice to others, even when it is not asked for. Probably it is the only thing that is freely given, as if it were a superfluous possession, has no use for us, and we want to get rid of it. We tell others how to live their lives, though our own may be far from exemplary. We want to improve others, our community, our society, and the world, though we do not understand ourselves, lack self-awareness and entertain no intention to develop our own inner strength.

What we do not appreciate is that only a flower that is blossoming can spread fragrance around, not one which is withered. We cannot spread light if our inner self is dark, and we cannot distribute milk or honey if our own bottle is dry. We want peace in the world, growth and development in our country so that we can prosper, but are filled with revenge, anger and enmity. The inner battles within us create great discord, agitation, and distress. The inner turmoil leads to depression, broken marriages, nervous breakdowns and substance abuse, etc. The weapons of mass destruction are not out there, but within us.

We want to modify the behaviour of all those close to us, but are not prepared to transform ourselves. Our focus is on others and never on ourselves. We pay attention to other peoples' mistakes, but find it difficult to acknowledge our own. In short, we know our spouse well, our brothers, sisters, friends, relatives well, we can narrate all their weaknesses and strengths, but never sit down to look deeply into our own inner strength.

Everything begins with the self. If you are at peace with yourself, others will recognise it and acknowledge it. If you exemplify good behaviour, lead a principled life based on high values, others will know it and possibly emulate it. Once you have conquered your own mind, you can then try to influence the world. The whole process starts with developing inner self through self-knowledge and mindfulness.

You can evolve gradually—it is a slow journey. But you can become what you are meant to be and find meaning and fulfilment. Once you have developed your inner strength, you will be like a deeply rooted tree that can stand in the strongest wind. It is because what you want is what you have consciously and carefully chosen. You will be calm and collected in difficult circumstances because through wisdom, the development of your self-awareness, the mind and spirit are fixed in higher values. This book aims to raise the reader's awareness, your awareness as to why peace of mind is eluding us. If you have an inner conflict and are not happy with 'how you are now', then perhaps you need to look at the contradictions. After pondering, if you decide to do something about the factors that are causing inner turmoil and undermining your peace of mind, then you are on the right road, ready to begin the long journey.

The second function or aim of this book is to affirm and foster hope since the human spirit can change. I strongly believe that we human beings have the potential and the capacity to change for the better.

Some people believe in being intrusive, in confronting others, and forcing them to see differently. They want to instil their own wisdom in others. This book is not about what to do, but it is to foster deep confidence in yourself, and to evoke that inner wisdom that guides you. It will not be instilling wisdom, but will endeavour to make you more reflective, so that you access the inner wisdom from your experience.

If you have faith in your self, and you change because you want to, then the change will endure. When we change because of somebody else's hectoring, the change may last for a few days, but it does not last. Raised awareness of 'Who I am' and 'How I am' could lead to happiness or contentment if you are living your life as you wish to live it. If we are true to ourselves, living a morally pure and virtuous life, then we should find inner peace. Inner conflict often arises from dissatisfaction with 'How I am' and how I want to be or could be.

You may want to map out a path of gradual change towards your inner world, your inner peace. The process may involve looking at your emotions, values, spirituality, and your sense of self and personal growth, your past, your present and your future. You may decide to amend or modify your values, your priorities or even opt for a major transformation. I hope this book will be a **companion** to you on the journey to attain inner peace and personal growth.

1

Our Search For Inner Peace

**Peace is not just the absence of sound.
It is the cool and quiet state of mind.**

If one had mystical powers and could hover around the world to ascertain how many people are living contented lives, at peace with themselves, the answer would be very few or hardly any. Guru Nanak, the founder of Sikhism who was born in 1466, said, "The whole world is troubled." We feel calm for a few minutes, happy when we get some material thing we have been longing for, but the sense of well-being does not last very long. We are rushing again and the quest for personal peace is sacrificed because we do not believe that this or that thing will be done on time or properly. We are hard on ourselves, and good at making other peoples' lives hell as well.

Some people report experiencing a slight peace for a short while after meeting or listening to a wise person or reading a serious book. When they get back to work, and the rest of their life, it is all gone. With others, the experience lasts only as long as the person is there for them or near them. When their 'guru' is no longer accessible, they revert to their old habits. Anyway, most of the so-called 'saintly persons' who profess to have miraculous powers have been exposed as fake or charlatans. Some groups are formed to find a peaceful orientation, but before long the members drift away and the 'club' comes to an end.

Bhagavad-Gita tells us that in life there are two paths: one is the path of attraction and the second one is the path of dedication. The path of attraction is gravitating towards whatever exerts a pull on us; it may be following our instincts, or our desires. We make choices which we can't really justify, but at the point of making a decision, we feel that is what we want to do.

The path of dedication is where we dedicate ourselves to a higher purpose. We take responsibilities for ourselves, but want to serve others as well. People who take the latter path are aware that we are on this Earth for bigger reasons than to eat, drink and be merry. Animals also eat, drink and reproduce. There is no harm in enjoying ourselves up to a certain extent, as long as it is within limits. One becomes dull when trying to refrain from all types of pleasures all the time. Ascetics practise self-discipline and abstain from all forms of pleasure. Ordinary people like us need to find a balance and think beyond the pleasures, aiming at a higher goal also.

Over-indulgence or hedonism leads to dissatisfaction and destruction. On the other hand pursuance of a higher goal leads to satisfaction and personal peace.

SELF

The whole objective of the human being is to free the personality from the contraction of self in desire into the expression of soul in love. (Rabindra Nath Tagore)

Donald Winniecott (1896–1971) distinguished between the 'true self' connected with the actual needs of each SUBJECT and the conformist or inauthentic 'false self' that arises out of the failure of the environment to support the true self. The self is the person's individuality or essence. When people say that he 'showed his true self', what they mean is that they had a glimpse of the most central part of the person. Self can be called the spirit or soul of the person. "The spirit is the true self." (De Republica Bk.) It is the deepest part of oneself that is somehow the same across different years and different experiences. If it is at the level of our spirit or soul, then it is our true identity. All other identities change, as they are not authentic—they are temporary.

Quite a few studies show that one of the factors which leads to crime is 'conformity'. Most of the offenders get into trouble with the law because they want to 'fit in' and do not want to be excluded from the group. We keep our mouth shut because we do not want to antagonise other members of a group especially if they are powerful people. 'Discretion is the better part of valour.' We agree with others without giving it a second thought, and spout their opinions freely.

We absorb different opinions till they become part of us. It is osmosis at work. We repeat what we have heard, students write it in their essays to get better marks, and the dislikes and likes of others become our likes and dislikes. Quite often I have heard even grown-ups say, "I don't like them because my mother doesn't like them."

Identification: In Social Psychology identification is the process of associating oneself closely with other individuals of Reference Groups to the extent that one comes to adopt their goals and values and to share vicariously their experiences. The Reference Groups could be the peer Group or your own family. The person is transformed in whole or part through taking aspects of the other.

I had to deal with a young man who was acutely depressed and wanted to be hospitalised. His explanation was that he had been adversely affected by a medicine he had been spraying in the fields for a relative of his. It had left him weak and lethargic. He had no wish to do anything at all. Even getting up in the mornings was a chore. When I talked to him, it became obvious that he had no goals, no aspirations and no substantive values of his own. His existence at that time centred round wanting to earn money, to please his parents. His happiness hinged on his Mom and Dad's approval. One of the factors leading to depression was his perceived fear that he could not fulfil their expectations.

For me as an individual, to be at peace with myself I have to confront myself, question myself about 'who I really am'. Am I authentic? If I have acquired a false identity through absorption, then the layers of false identity acquired over the years have to be discarded. Only through a process of rigorous examination can contact with the true 'true self' be made. Self-analysis on a regular basis could lead us to be true to ourselves. If we are true to ourselves, then it will be difficult to be false to others. If there is self-acceptance, then others will accept you as well, as you are.

ACCEPT YOURSELF

Too Many people overvalue what they are not, and undervalue what they are.

If in your mind, you see yourself as unacceptable amongst your colleagues at your workplace, your friends and relationships; it will eventually manifest itself in reality. It is difficult to find personal peace if we do not accept ourselves as we are. Once we accept ourselves as we are, then we can chart our development and endeavour to realise our human potential. Accepting ourselves involves not only accepting our strengths, but our weaknesses as well. It is difficult to be at peace with oneself when so much social emphasis is placed on feeling good, getting ahead and having the best. Such expectations indeed make it difficult to accept oneself as one is.

In the Far East, or collectivist societies, up to a certain measure, identity is still conferred by class, gender, and family. Though people do relocate away from their town or village of birth, their identity is still linked to their background, though their personal achievements or failures also influences the sense of their identity. There has been a shift from the collectivist to individualist society in the West in the last 50 years. In the individualist society, notably in the English speaking nations, identity is achieved or one tries to 'discover' who you are. You create your own social milieu that is separate from your childhood one. Most people move away from the place of birth and their family for educational or work opportunities.

Anyway, whatever your background, you can accept others only if you have accepted yourself—who you are in your workplace, in your life. The mind can easily dwell upon negative aspects of oneself or other people. This is the easiest way of looking at life, as it is actually difficult to be kind to yourself, to like yourself. We always say that we should be kind to others—"Treat thy neighbour as thyself." We can treat others with love and kindness only if we are positive about ourselves, calm and mindful of our thoughts and feelings.

When we do not accept ourselves, we feel there is something lacking, something inherently bad, something to be ashamed of, or not measuring up to a standard we have in our minds. The self-acceptance that we deny ourselves is based on our own judgement, our own standards which we hold. We are our own worst critics, our own worst enemies. We feel angry or hurt when someone criticises us because it may be approximating what we are already feeling or thinking. If you believe that you deserve to go to a higher realm in life, to achieve your full potential, you will take positive steps to achieve that goal. If on the other hand, you do not accept yourself, you will not have the drive to realize your vision. The drive must come from within. If you do not believe in yourself, the changes you want to make, the goals you want to achieve will seem huge and overwhelming. If whatever you want to achieve is your choice, and you believe that you deserve your vision, you will change your internal world and your life.

We know what nurtures the heart—it is Truth, calmness, compassion and loving kindness, contentment, and the wisdom to distinguish right from wrong. When people are kind to us or present themselves as genuinely caring, peace arises in our hearts. We feel peaceful and calmer. This is what we can do with ourselves also. Be kind and compassionate to ourselves. If by extension, we all do this to one another, the world will be a more calm and peaceful place. So if you cultivate kindness and infinite patience towards yourself, accept yourself as you are, be yourself whether at work or at home,—no need for pretence, for acting, in a certain way in public and another way in private; you will have a high level of integration.

Whatever happens in life, successes and setbacks, highs and troughs, achievements and mistakes are all part of the process, the journey of life, but not the whole **YOU.** If we are not kind to ourselves, not able to forgive ourselves when mistakes are made, it will be difficult to improve and nurture the dream we have.

There is no need to become inactive or complacent when practising acceptance. You are observing,—what is—and once you have accepted it, you devise strategies to attain what you want. You become more pro-active, as you do not dwell on the past but think more of where you want to be. Acceptance also enables us to be proud of our good qualities, our values, and to let go of what you can't control. We learn to make do with what we have, and know what we need to acquire. We feel stressed or disappointed when things do not go our way. Acceptance enables you to let go of what you can't control, and do something about your **Circle of Influence** or what is within your control.

To accept ourselves, we need to know who we are. Make a time to answer the question, Who Am I? Reflect on it. With self-awareness, one can feel confident about one's beliefs and identity and share them without fear of embarrassment and ridicule.

NATURE AND NURTURE

No one is our enemy; no one is a stranger to us. We have befriended the whole world
(Guru Granth Sahib)

We are all a product of two factors, nature and nurture. Each one of us is born with a distinct personality, a distinctive character or qualities. Our personality is the integrated organisation of all the psychological, intellectual, emotional and physical characteristics. We all have traits and qualities which are good and bad, nice and ugly. Some of these characteristics make us socially attractive and others do not. So when you understand that a person is a product of his nature, and may not even be aware of deep-rooted traits, inherent tendencies, or shortcomings, you accept the person as she or he is. **When you suspend your judgement you are at peace with yourself.**

When we see a person with a tendency to be angry all the time, we need to understand that the person is a victim of their nature or nurture. You will be at peace and probably happier if you try to identify their strengths rather than their shortcomings. When you manifest a tendency to understand people, accept them as they are, they are at ease with you. They feel cared for, appreciated, and they will co-operate with you. You will have people you can work with, talk with, and motivated people around you.

So how do we refine our feelings so that hatred does not creep into our minds, so that we can co-exist with our in-laws and the boss who keeps getting at you? Row[1] offers very practical advice when she says: "A person is crude and ill mannered because he has been denied the requisite training that you have been privy to. Given the right education, he would be as refined as you are. A cultured person is also a product of careful cultivation of fine qualities. When you understand this, your attitude towards both the crude and refined person remains the same."

SOME IDEAS TO THINK ABOUT

- **When you hate, your mind is not at peace. YOU suffer and not the person you hate.**

- **If the Creator is the same, then the same spirit, the same spark runs in all of us.**

- **We see differences and not the humanity of others. This is the bane of our existence.**

---

1.   See Row, J. (2007), *Profile of the Perfect Person,* Mumbai, Jaico Publishing House.

FULLEST DEVELOPMENT

An important feature of a good life in Aristotle's view is that it should involve a concern for others. He distinguishes genuine friendship from two superficially similar kinds of acquaintanceship, one in which the basis of the relationship is pleasure, and the other in which it is mutual usefulness. The shallow forms of friendship last only as long as the pleasure or utility they afford, whereas true friendship lasts because it is grounded in 'good', in the sense that one wishes for one's friend what is best for him or her. Aristotle calls this friendship 'perfected or completed' because its goal lies within the relationship itself, and does not treat it as merely instrumental for some other or further end.

Aristotle says that a friend is 'another self', meaning that the kind of concern one properly has for one's own good is extended to one's friend too. Proper self-concern is appropriate for an ethical individual who will be motivated thereby to *act nobly*, and to make intelligent decisions about how to choose and act. Such an individual will always see as a social being, that what is best for him is at one with what is best for his friends and eventually for the community as well. Thus to treat a friend as another self, is always to wish the best for her, for her own sake, and to act accordingly.

People are essentially social creatures, which means that the attainment of tranquillity of mind cannot take place other than in a social setting. Reciprocally, the well being of society depends on that of its members. The community's interests do not outweigh or negate individual interests; they are intertwined and must be fostered together. As an individual is an organic part of his or her society, so an individual flourishing cannot be detached from the flourishing of the community. The fullest development of each individual is dependent upon the well being of others.

SELF WORTH

Self worth is self-appreciation, being compassionate to yourself and recognising your internal abundance. Internal abundance is appreciating that you are worthy of your life, you have potential for growth mentally and emotionally and physically. Your everyday struggles offer you the opportunity to grow spiritually. You recognise that you have a purpose in life and a responsibility to have a meaningful life. If you believe in Higher Power, then you will also recognise that all human beings have been created by the same Creator and all human beings are equal. We are one family.

A person with low esteem might think, "I don't deserve that job"—and might not pursue the dream job. Persons with low esteem may not ask for a pay rise or leave an abusive relationship because they accept what comes their way. When they are working towards a goal, they might give it up relatively early because they believe that they don't have what it takes or deserve to be successful. Such people might even sacrifice their own well being to please others, because they need others' approval. In short, they do not accept themselves as they are.

If you value yourself, you are unlikely to be craving for recognition, attention, external power or influence over others, because no matter how much you gain by way of power, status, etc., the need for more is always there. The external cravings are like the receding horizon that you cannot reach, no matter how fast you travel. Scarcity of self-value cannot be remedied by wealth, influence, recognition or status.

If you do not value yourself adequately, please ask yourself:

- Why do you feel that you are worth less than any other person?

- Do you think that you have a shortage of talents, good looks, money, etc? (Write them down.)

HELP SUGGESTIONS

1. By being mindful, observe your thoughts about not having enough of.... (Your answer to the above question.)

2. Consider each item from a new perspective. Ask yourself: Is it my self-value that is lacking or **what I think** is lacking in terms of these items?

3. Consider the possibility that you are a valuable person. You do not have to internalise the labels that other people try to attach to you, i.e. useless, ugly, good for nothing, too young, too old, over the hill, etc.

4. Write down all your good qualities, your strengths. Include all the good things you are engaged in at present—voluntary work, helping a colleague at work, etc.

5. When you focus on your strengths, you see yourself as a competent person, a person with self esteem because your goals in life and strengths are aligned. You are at ease, comfortable in your own skin.

6. Develop a new perspective, one that is based on your strengths and reality.

7. Be true to yourself. **Stand up for your values.**

8. Explore where you are now—and where you want to be. Identify your own unique calling in life. Each one of us has some deeply embedded interest, or talent. If you identify that, you will find a higher ideal in that field. Make an Action Plan and carry it out.

TOP TIPS

• The sun warms all and does not require appreciation. What is stopping you from radiating like a sun?

• Shakespeare said in Hamlet, "What a piece of work is a man! How noble in reason! How infinite in faculty, in apprehension, how like a god." You can be a noble soul too if you subscribe to higher values.

• 'As you think so you become'. The trick is constantly to think about who you are now, and who you want to become. With mindfulness, you can identify the skills, or your learning needs to achieve your goals. Once you are immersed in what you want in your life, the characteristics you value, your negative thoughts about yourself will be squeezed out.

RECOGNISE THE GOOD THINGS

Science is now proving that feeling grateful for the things we have can actually make us healthier. Practising gratitude, acknowledging the blessings in our lives and making it a point to recognise the good things can change us positively. We will feel better if we practise this over a long period of time; we will realise that we are making progress towards our life goals—especially of our search for peace.

Robert Emmons, a lecturer in psychology at the University of California, and psychologist Michael McCullough of the University of Miami, took three groups of volunteers and randomly assigned them to focus on one of three things each week: hassles, things for which they were grateful and ordinary life events. The first group concentrated on everything that went wrong or was annoying to them, such as "too much traffic on the road." The second group focused on things that enhanced their lives, such as: "I have a very nice family. I am lucky to have such lovely kind people." The third group thought of recent things they had done, as in, "I went shopping on Friday morning and …"

Their finding was that people who focused on gratitude were much happier. They saw their lives in favourable terms. They spent almost an hour and a half more per week exercising than those who focused on hassles. Plainly, those who were grateful had a higher quality of life. In a follow-up study, the results showed that those who found something to appreciate every day were less materialistic, in the sense that they were less apt to see a connection between life satisfaction and material things. They were more willing to part with their material things.

So to generate good feelings, reach out to others. A gesture towards other individuals, a genuine, warm 'Thank You' costs you little, but can bring many benefits. Gratitude expressed to others usually comes back round. It has a boomerang effect. People who feel appreciated are more willing to make an effort for those who make them valued.

Scientists say that good feelings generated by gratitude help in the release of dopamine, the chemical in the brain associated with happiness. Dopamine is released when people are feeling good or are excited by a challenge. It activates the part of the brain in which complex thinking and conflict resolution are thought to be based.

So to take advantage of the 'feel good factor,' just before bedtime, jot down three things that happened that day that you are grateful for. Anything that made you uplifted, that brought a smile to your face or your heart or will contribute to your future happiness. It could be a telephone call from an old friend, the face of an elderly relative when you last visited her or the smooth journey to your place of destination. (No traffic!)

Such a journal will make you look at life differently, in a positive, appreciative way, reminding you that we are living in an exciting, invigorating and interesting place where we are all interconnected. It forces you to look at what went right instead of the hassles and things that went wrong. It enhances your self-esteem.

BRINGING NEW CHARACTERISTICS INTO YOUR LIFE

Think of three characteristics YOU WANT TO INTRODUCE INTO YOUR LIFE. They could be self-esteem, tranquillity and compassion, or others like confidence, courage, bravery, etc., which you value. Ask yourself:

1.   How would someone with that characteristic look like?

2.   How would I feel around someone with that characteristic?

3.   What would having someone with that characteristic mean to me?

4.   How can I bring the trait into my life and nurture it?

5.   What do I need to change in order to have more compassion, self-esteem and tranquillity?

SHOWING AND EARNING RESPECT

Respect is the foundation of all strong relationships. Quite often we nurture the delusion that respect can be gained by a title, position, wealth, or even age. Older people expect people younger than them to show them respect. As a matter of fact, we should learn to respect people older than us not only because of their age, but also because of their experience and wisdom. However, older people need to demonstrate that they are worthy of respect. People who want to be respected should not expect that it is their right; it has to be earned.

If you want to respect others, you have to nurture self-respect. As it is within, so it is without. You can't have the respect and trust of others if they perceive you to be dishonest, unreliable or untrustworthy. The key is to respect others consistently as you would like to be respected.

Some people want respect, yet fail to provide others with the same trust or respect. It is not a one-way street—it has to be mutual. Even small gestures that tell others that they are important, that you respect their individuality, can make all the difference in the world.

True respect is earned by the display of solid ethical character. Your real strength and influence as a father, mother or line manager lie in relating to your family and staff with respect for who they are, for their humanity. If you order your child to obey your commands, the child may superficially comply with your wishes, but there will be no cheerfulness or zeal in the compliance. Their verbal communications will be manifesting passive aggressive behaviour such as indifference, sulkiness, apathy or half-heartedness, pouting, etc. An employee treated with disrespect often responds with resistance and resentment. You may win the battle but lose the war.

USEFUL HINTS

- Model what you preach.

- If you want to have a positive influence on people you normally interact with—friends, relatives, colleagues—ask of yourself what you ask of them.

- Respect them first and then be respected.

- If you refrain from criticizing others, in all probability they will return the favour.

- When you assert the superiority of your ways over others, that is **domination.** When you value others' views as your own, that is **respect.**

LISTENING TO UNDERSTAND

When we listen with patience and appreciation, even when we disagree, we are choosing respect and love. Flexible people have a genuine desire to understand and look for constructive and positive aspects. When we judge somebody with fear and doubt, we concentrate on destructive and negative characteristics. With mindfulness, we can be aware of our thoughts, words and actions that come from fear and instead choose to act out of love and respect for others. When we listen with patience and appreciation of the other person's views, we show respect. In a conversation a mindful person aims to listen, to understand, and then to act on it.

When we listen with a view to understand, we absorb the person's ideas for consideration. We are not thinking of the party we are attending, or how to shut up the person so that we can have our say. (Unless the person is very loquacious!) When we cultivate a genuine desire to understand, we are receptive, and then we see beyond appearances. Our attention is on the essence of what the person wants to convey and not on gender, race, clothes, jewellery, etc. Our judgement is suspended and our heart opens.

Sometimes we think that our path is the right one, and we want others to agree with us. The more you want others to follow your way, the less open you are to what they think, feel, and believe. Your agenda is to change them, so they cannot really talk with you because you are not listening. It also happens that when some of us are stressed, we tune out other people completely. Some people find it difficult to listen to what others are telling them at the precise moments when they most need to do so. The lack of self-control sabotages our ability to listen and empathise with people. With mindfulness, you can tune in to the sensations of your body so that you can monitor yourself for early warning signs that you are about to feel upset or fly off the handle or launch into a harangue. You can use the day-to-day events as the laboratory for learning to improve your listening skills and empathy. Try taking the following four steps:

1. Step back—listen, don't jump in.

2. Let the other person finish whatever he or she is saying.

3. Try to be objective—ask yourself, 'Is there a sound reason for my reactions, or am I being too hasty in jumping to conclusions?'

4. Ask clarifying questions rather than ones that sound hostile or judgemental.

With small changes, we can empathise and listen, understand the other person's views more fully, and have a rational dialogue. We do not have to agree with the other person, but give the person a chance to have his or her say. Once you allow yourself to listen, understand and empathise, you can let them know what your thoughts are and they would be more receptive.

POSITIVE ACCEPTANCE OF MARRIAGE OR RELATIONSHIP

Unhappiness and dissatisfaction in our lives involves wishing that some things were different. Accepting the current situation is called 'positive acceptance.' Once we have accepted the status quo, we can move onto thinking, "How can I improve it?"

Researchers say that the key to a happy marriage is accepting that at times relationships will be difficult and at times painful. Therapists claim that 'mindful acceptance' of family rows, shouting, and ranting is better than believing in perfect marriage.

The other extreme of the spectrum is that there are people who are nervous about getting married or entering into long-term relationships, as they believe that they do not last. We all know of couples, whether in relationships or married who do not trust each other and feel very insecure. It s not uncommon for people to employ private detectives to check on their partners, especially when they suspect them of having an affair. Others keep tabs on their partners discreetly and sometimes not so discreetly too. Such couples live together but there is no bond, no real understanding, and no progression in the marital life or relationship.

In the present-day culture, when we are expected to be positive all the time, and in the 'can do' spirit, some people believe that they can achieve a state of domestic bliss. Other couples present themselves as happy couples in public, but delve a little bit into their lives and you will find suspicion lurking in every corner. The façade of perfection, of a happy couple, covers a mess of resentment and suffering.

Mindful acceptance, says the *Journal of Marital and Family Therapy*, is the realization that while some pain is inevitable, the suffering of the struggle against things we cannot change is not. We all need to be realistic and accept that there is a darker side to life also. We all chase happiness, **but true well-being is not about the pursuit of a permanent state of happiness**. It involves helping family members work together to negotiate their way through difficult times and sharing the good times. If there are difficulties, differences can be worked through calmly.

Couples often descend into classical symptoms of impending divorce or separation such as shouting rather than listening to understand, mutual reproach, a lack of respect and a constant habit of belittling one another, calling names, etc. If you catch it early enough, you can often prevent this sort of disease developing any further. With the right emotional tools and good will, differences can be resolved.

A spouse or a partner is a special friend, too. Aristotle distinguishes genuine friendship from two types of superficial acquaintanceship, 'one in which the basis of the relationship is pleasure, the other in which it is mutual usefulness.' These shallow forms of friendship last as long as the pleasure or utility they offer. True friendship lasts because it is grounded in good, in the sense that one wishes for one's friend what is best for him or her. Aristotle says that a friend is 'another self' meaning that the kind of concern one properly has for one's own good is extended to one's friend also.

The same advice can be applied to relationships or a marriage also. A relationship is not merely an instrumental good, but has intrinsic value. Its pleasure derives from not only what one spouse can do for each other and give each other, but in disinterested and altruistic actions as well. In an ideal relationship, the partner is supposed to be a friend where the friendship is mutual and personal. It involves sharing activities, discussing issues and actions, co-operating and supporting one another. The capacities of each other will be enhanced.

In such a relationship, there is striving towards a better or happier union, a shared endeavour to better themselves, a desire for measurable achievement and greatness. The satisfaction of reaching spiritual or artistic milestones is their main concern.

However, it must be acknowledged also that not every couple is compatible, and when the prognosis is complete separation or full blown divorce, ensure that the other party keep their dignity and emerge feeling calm rather than in pieces. There is no need to stab the other partner in the back or poison the atmosphere. People tend to blame the other party, but it takes two to scupper a marriage. Each partner needs to acknowledge that they both had a role to play in the breakdown of the marriage. If one has an affair, the other person has to ask himself or herself what it was about his or her behaviour that caused it to happen

AFFAIRS—PLATONIC LOVE

Affairs happen in every society; the difference may be in degree, in some places they are prevalent, and in others not so prevalent. In some societies affairs are a big taboo, hence indulged in with great discreetness and in others they are part of life. When affairs are found out, and mostly they are, they cause enormous pain, distress and financial loss—if they lead to separation or divorce. Infidelity is often given as the reason for divorce in courts.

As far as emotional impact is concerned, some women have panic attacks every time their partner walks out of the house or comes home late. There is no trust. Relationships and marriages are based on trust. Husbands or males too feel very insecure and become violent if they suspect their partners to be less than 100 per cent loyal. History is replete with wars and acts of violence against others just because a man had a rival and wanted to have the woman he fancied.

Advances in technology are giving cheating individuals new ways to be unfaithful. Most of the people who have an affair do it by mobile. But gone are the days when the little woman at home didn't have her own source of income. As women now are independent, they don't have to put up with their partner's behaviour just to have a roof over their head or food for her children. Sooner or later they reach a point where they feel strong enough to handle the truth. They are not prepared to accept infidelity. A survey in June 2007 of divorce lawyers found that 49 percent in Britain who suspect their partner of having an affair use a private investigator (PI) to confirm their suspicions.

At the risk of being accused of being too puritanical, I would like to say it is better to avoid sexual liaisons outside of your marriage or relationship. The reality is that in the current climate of sexually transmitted infections, one cannot be careful enough. It is common knowledge that sexually transmitted infections are on the rise. You may be free of the disease, but what about the other person? You may have slept with your spouse only, but the other person might have slept with two other people, and the two might have slept with ten others.

It is also worth remembering that it takes only a minute's carelessness for the infidelity to be discovered. A client of mine found incriminating texts in his partners mobile. Another found intimate letters hidden in a chest of drawers. Sexual betrayal can feel like an emotional juggernaut crashing into your heart, stomach and brain. It's naïve to expect the betrayed party to shake it off easily. It can take months and even years for the wounds to heal and for life to settle back to anywhere normal. Lurking suspicion as to whether the person you live with can be trusted will be latent or in the subconscious and can surface even when innocuous statements are made or things happen.

As well as the usual health hazards, what you gain from an affair is very small compared to what you risk losing. If you are tempted to have an affair just for enjoyment, look at the whole relationship and not a few perceived shortcomings in your spouse and ask yourself if it is worth saving or not? List all the good points in the relationship.

People say that the sensuous appetite is not always easy to control. We read and hear scandals about some icons, sports heroes, and public figures practically every day. Even some very highly venerated sages and saints have succumbed to the lusts of the flesh. In the absence of proper moral code, or any clear consensus on sexual morality, people have to decide whatever is right or wrong for themselves. Quite often it is a struggle between lust and will, passion and fidelity. If people find themselves in such a dilemma, and find self-control slipping, they might wish to ponder on the following questions before having a fling:

- If you are married or cohabiting, put yourself in the shoes of your life partner. How would your partner feel? What would the partner think about you? What will the partner do?

- Is the affair compatible with your higher values?

- What is your life going to be if you split up—worse or better?

SOME SUGGESTIONS TO THINK ABOUT

1. Do not take your partner for granted. Take him or her seriously.

2. Openly discuss if there are any problems in the marriage or relationship and how it can be improved.

3. Write down three things you could improve about yourself. When you take responsibility and take concrete steps to make changes, hopefully your partner will do the same and catch your sincerity. **Recognising your responsibility is a virtue.**

Now let us see what Plato the famous Greek philosopher has to say about this issue. A characteristic feature of Plato's outlook was his sharp division between things intellectual and things of the senses and in particular between rational temperance and sensuality. He clearly implied that rational temperance is preferable to sensuality. He argued in *The Symposium* that the best kind of love should not express itself physically, but intellectually only, a conception commonly known as 'Platonic love'. Platonic love or friendship is purely spiritual, not sexual. People well acquainted with this subject have often discussed whether a nonsexual relationship is possible between a man and a woman. You, the reader, may wish to reflect on it, but this was Plato's personal morality.

We can love others as much as we like, but love does not have to give into plea-sure of the senses or lust. It can be platonic love. Guru Amardas (Guru Nanak 3) enjoined his followers thus:

Another person's property, another man's wife,
Talking ill of another, poisons one's life.

PERFECT FORM OF BEAUTY

Plato, besides talking about the internal justices or the conception of harmony, also advances the idea of a justly lived life. In his view a justly lived life is a hap-pier one than an unjustly lived life. By this Plato does not mean a life lived according to a balanced arrangement of reason and the passions—it is a life of proportion. Without a sense of internal justice, or proportion, one will not be able to set a limit to one's desires and will therefore be discontented. Plato believed that a person who reflects on his or her life in order to make it balanced, will know that the pleasures of the mind far outweigh those of the body. Accord-ing to Bhagvad Gita, pleasures of the mind are superior to the pleasures of the body, and the pleasures of the intellect are superior to the pleasures of the mind.

Plato also believed that there is a sharp division between reason and the appetites, between things intellectual and things of the senses—which really means between rational temperance and sensuality. He argued in *Symposium* that the best kind of love should not express itself physically, but should be expressed intellectually only. It is a conception commonly known as 'Platonic love'. Put simply, Platonic love is purely spiritual and not sexual.

This reveals a different outlook to the one we are used to in modern society, where lust and self-indulgence are encouraged. Plato, on the other hand, had a sharp division between reason and appetites, between things intellectual and things of the senses, and clearly favoured temperance and not sensuality.

It is said that Ghalib who was considered a top poet in India during his time kept on looking at a famous female singer who used to sing at the king's court. Even-tually she approached him and asked him if he was aware of the consequences were she to report the matter to the king. His asked her: 'Who says I was looking at you?' He recited a poem in Urdu, but in short his response was to the effect that he was not looking at her *per se*, but at God's creation. If true, it was a poetic or sublime response indeed.

There is beauty within us all, a treasure in our depths. However, we are too busy looking at the outer self only. The outer mask is deceptive; we should allow the energy within us to shine.

The Greek philosopher also describes an ascent through stages of love, from passion for an individual's body, to love of beauty wherever manifested in the physical world, thence to the love of the beauty of the soul as something higher than physical beauty, and then by way of love for life and different kinds of knowledge, to love of the eternal and perfect Form of Beauty itself from which all beautiful things get their nature.

"GOOD LIFE"

Quite often a philosophical question prods us about a good life and we find most people discussing the place of wealth in life. People discuss the difficult question for a short while as A.C. Grayling says in *What Is Good?* : "Iterating platitudes (which they widely ignore in practice) about money as such not bringing happiness or fulfilment. If we look into classical antiquity, the contemporaries of the Greek philosopher, Socrates, observed that wealth, pleasure, or wisdom were the chief ingredients of happiness. For Socrates however, happiness consists in what he described 'as the perfection of soul'."

Socrates devoted his energies to asking questions about what constitutes the good life and he put his question in his own unique way: "Is there a goal, a purpose, a value in life which is worthwhile as an end in itself and not merely as a means to other things?" What principally mattered to Socrates was 'the quest itself, the quest for ethical living' rather than the conclusion he or anyone came to. Perhaps his thinking was that even though the ideals suggested by such a quest are in practice unattainable, the life of striving for them is itself the 'good life.'

In the *Republic*, Plato states that an ideal city state is one in which each of the community's three orders of citizens—the governors, the 'guardians' or military men, and the general population, do what is appropriate for their position in society, and thereby preserve the balance or social harmony. Similarly, just as a city state has three components necessary for social harmony, an individual has three parts: reason, the emotions and appetites. When they are in harmony, the individual is happy. Achieving internal harmony is, according to Socrates and written by Plato, 'the object of an intelligent man's life.' (Plato was a student of Socrates.)

Plato argues that an individual who lives justly will know, as a result of reflecting on his life in order to make it balanced and harmonious, which pleasures are true pleasures and which ones are not. Such a person will know that the pleasures of the mind far outweigh those of the body.

The debate whether man is rational or irrational has continued since Aristotle. Like animals, human beings, move about, perceive and have desires. But the defining mark or essence of man is that he is rational. To be human is to reason—to think by employing practical reason in how to live. Aristotle's view is that it behoves the moral agent to determine from the facts of a case, what is the right course of action in that case. The person in that situation should do the sensible thing, based on practical wisdom or prudence. Since the good life for man is the life lived in accordance **with his essence**, it follows that the good life for an individual is a life of 'practical wisdom'. If one cannot oneself be practically wise, one should imitate those who are.

In Aristotle's view a good life or a virtuous life should involve concern for others. The very highest ideal of the life though was reserved for contemplation by Aristotle. Contemplation is thought and study for its own sake. He writes:

"We ought not to listen to those who counsel us to think as mere mortals should think, and to remember our mortality. Rather we ought to strive towards attaining something great, and leave nothing un-attempted in the effort to live conformably (consistent) with the highest thing in us. Our rationality might be modest in quantity but in power and value it outstrips everything else about us. We may indeed believe this is a man's true self, being the sovereign and best part of him."

INNER STRENGTH

We need to fight injustice outwardly, but at the same time we have to find ways to cope inwardly, ways to train our minds to remain calm and not develop frustration, hatred or despair. At work also, we have to maintain a feeling of calmness and inner satisfaction in an environment that is focused on meeting selfish ends, i.e. profits, volume of production, etc.

To reshape one's attitude with deep and sustained reflection, is not easy, and it takes time. There is a reason why it is sometimes a long and a difficult process to reshape our attitudes and outlook, to change the habitual ways in which we perceive the world. We are accustomed to our customary interpretation and response to any situation, that others can even predict what it will be. To modify such habits, requires repeated effort and mindfulness. Many of us resist giving up our misery.

To build inner strength is sometimes like weeding a garden. You need to get rid of the weeds that are choking out the plants you are trying to grow. The mind does its own things or, should we say, the mind has its own mind! Potential obstacles to your personal growth are inevitable. Getting rid of old habits, or to change the obnoxious patterns, is not easy—but it has to be done, otherwise they will destroy what you have planted.

HOW TO BUILD INNER STRENGTH

1. We may find help in our belief system, faith in God, or we can use our intelligence to analyse the situation and to see it from a different perspective.

2. Use our human reason to shape our attitude and outlook.

3. Questioning oneself whether responding with anger or jealousy, for instance, will benefit or harm us in the long run. We have to reflect deeply on whether responding in this way brings a happier and more peaceful state of mind, or if these emotions make us unhappy.

4. Think about how others will respond to you when you show frustration, anger, or jealousy. Think: Will it improve my relationship? Will it better or spoil my relationship?

5. Think of similar experiences in the past and the consequences. Carry on reflecting/meditating on these lines till you are convinced about the futility of responding to situations with hostility, and or revenge as a motive.

CONTEMPLATION

Most wise men and philosophers give a lot of prominence to contemplation, in the sense of thought and study for its own sake. The life of contemplation is a good life because it is an activity which can lead to change and inner well-being. By contemplation is meant philosophical enquiry where you survey with your mind or with your eyes. Most of us give up studying serious works after school or university. If reason is the highest feature of human kind, and its possession our most distinguishing mark, then it follows that it has to be cultivated, so that we can express our essence in the most fitting way.

Aristotle says, "We ought to strive towards attaining something great, and leave nothing unattempted in the effort to live conformably with the highest thing in us. Our rationality might be modest in quantity but in power and value, it outstrips everything else about us."

PEACE IN THE HOME

In my book, *Achieving a Balanced Healthy Life*, I wrote about being more assertive in everyday interactions and not to hesitate to say 'No' if you consider that you are asked to act in ways incompatible with your dignity or self-esteem. Assertiveness is standing up for your rights. Knowing what you feel is not enough; you must let the other party know to have emotional freedom. So assertive behaviour is: "Knowing your rights, and doing something about it, and doing this within the framework of emotional freedom." Fensterheim and Baer say in *Don't say Yes when you want to say No*, that the criterion for assertive behaviour is: "if you have doubts whether a specific act was assertive, ask yourself if it increased your self respect even slightly. If it did, it was assertive. If it did not, it was unassertive."

As far as your relationship or marriage is concerned, there is no need to assert yourself at every opportunity. It can be counter productive. Swami says, "In a marriage, one of the biggest keys to success is surrender." We expend so much energy and time fighting with our partners or spouses, that we are hardly left with any time to show our affection. Arguments are fine, as long as they do not escalate into a fight. Normally they escalate because we do not want to give in, but want everything to be done 'my way.' Sometime we fear that if I let go of the argument it will make me appear small. The little time we have with our families need not be wasted in battles of the will. It requires maturity and self-confidence to appreciate that we do not have to win every argument. You look after your partner's well being and retain your sanity when you do not insist on having 'your way'.

If you win an argument, what do you really gain? A moment's satisfaction probably, but at what cost? It would probably be at the expense of causing pain, anger and feelings of resentment in your partner or spouse.

If you lead a life free of conflict, you deserve to be congratulated. If however it is not that peaceful in the domestic sphere, then please try to answer the following questions honestly:

- Do arguments normally start because of your ego?

- How can you control your ego or urge to have it 'your way?

- Is your way really better than his or her way?

- What will you gain if you win the argument?

INTERDEPENDENCE

A relationship or marriage is built on interdependence. You can be truly independent and at the same time have a relationship truly based on interdependence. It requires maturity and self-awareness to know when you are trying to control your spouse or partner.

If you consider that the issue under discussion is important, then go for a win-win outcome. We like to think that 'My way is the correct one, and others must agree with me.' You don't have to coerce or dominate your spouse, but look for a solution that is acceptable to both of you.

HUMANITY

They give diverse impressions because of the varieties of forms and ways of different countries.
All human beings have the same eyes, the same ears, and the same form of body.
And each body is composed of the same elements....
(Guru Granth Sahib)

We all like to play with babies because they are innocent. A baby will come to you in complete trust, irrespective of your gender, race colour or background. The baby comes with a clean slate and is not conscious of any differences or distinctions. Parents, peers and significant others write on the slate and imprint their prejudices.

Kang Youwei—a Chinese philosopher—identified nine types of distinctions which generate various forms of suffering. I think the following six are very relevant in this era: Nationality, class, race, physical form (especially female and male), family distinctions and occupation. We also look upon people with a different religion or value system different from us with suspicion. Kang envisioned a worldwide Utopia without political, social, economic, racial or sexual distinctions, and the strife that follows from such distinctions.

In Sikh history, Bhai Kanayha tended to the wounded in battle on both sides. He was reported to Guru Gobind Singh, the tenth Guru of the Sikhs. When questioned by the Guru, Bhai Kanayha said that he does not see any distinction between friend and foe. Everyone appears the same to him, as we all have been created by the same Creator. Guru Gobind Singh realized that Bhai Kanayha had risen above ordinary considerations like 'my people and others,' enmity, and saw the same humanity in everyone. He was delighted with the answer and gave him more bandages and medicines.

If we 'Recognise the whole of Humanity as equal', the world will definitely be a much more peaceful place.

SERVICE TO OTHERS

Service to others is an ideal advocated by most world religions. Personal advancement is fine but as members of the human race we have a larger set of duties as well. If possible, the service needs to be rendered without expectation of reward and if it is really selfless, it counteracts egoism. Service done as a labour of love frees those actively involved in it from greed, pride and undue worldly attachments. At our workplace or in our personal life, service denotes attention to duty in all spheres of life according to ability and capacity also.

Service can be of three types. It can be done with what people in Punjabi call Tan (body—manual service) Dhan (money—material service) and Man (mind—intellectual service).

Mother (St) Teresa who founded the Missionaries of Charity helped abandoned children in Calcutta with her body, mind and heart. She won the Nobel Prize in 1979 for her salutary service. Her nuns in their distinctive sari-like habit are to be found all over the world working with the poorest in the country. People all over the world make donations to such good causes or charitable organisations.

Service, like charity, can begin at home. We look at elderly people as a burden and forget the contribution they have made to their family, their community and society in general. We ignore the fact that they too have hopes, and dreams. If we want to be of service to them, then we need to look beyond their frailty and occasional eccentricities and recognise their humanity. They may still have a big contribution to make in view of their wisdom and experience.

In Sikh Gudwaras, the Langar (Community kitchen) is a place of charity and service, where each gives according to his capacity and takes according to her needs. The devotees pay for expenses, bring provisions, and personally contribute their labour and time by cooking the food, cleaning the utensils and serving food. It is thought meritorious to take meals in a langar with others rising above sectarian prejudices, and mixing like a family without differentiation of social, political or spiritual status. Though it is changing now in western countries, traditionally all who visited the Gurdwara sat in rows (pangat) on mats symbolizing equality when partaking of the food.

Unfortunately, while doing some form of service, people often veer to the opposite side of the spectrum and lose the plot. The primary aim of being of service to others is abandoned and instead it is carried out to boost the ego. It is no longer unselfish, without the desire for any praise, flattery or prestige. Instead of counteracting their egoism it enlarges it. I have seen people engaged in voluntary service come to blows because they become attached to the 'titles' or power or the 'chair'. Such individuals expend considerable amounts of energy and money as well to be elected to a certain position, especially the post of 'president.' It becomes a badge of honour for them, and their identity. Service is no longer selfless, it is not to help others, but it is for self-aggrandizement. The service is no longer genuine, but instrumental in their desire for power or status. They have large egos which require constant nurturing.

"I put for a general inclination of all mankind, a perpetual and restless desire for power after power that ceaseth only in death."—Leviathan (1651)

I am not even for a second implying that we should not serve on different voluntary organisations or charitable trusts. I have held different positions in sports and voluntary organisations and they have been a great source of satisfaction and fulfilment for me. As members of the Community or society we need to realize that we have a large set of duties and responsibilities that transcend personal concerns. As part of personal growth, we all need to have a sense of personal growth.

However, when we try to live a 'good life', to help others, we need to be aware what it entails. "How shall I live a good life?" is asked quite often by individuals. You need to search within you, for the best way for you to serve and live.

The following questions can be useful in reaching the right decision:

- What is your motivation for doing the service?

- Do you have any ulterior motives?

- What will be your thoughts if you do not get the recognition you feel you justly deserve?

- Will the service which you intend to provide be ultimately of benefit or harm to others and you?

- Are you doing the service to sustain your pride or because you genuinely want to help others?

IT IS US AGAINST THEM

A devotee is: "One who hates no being" (Bhavad Gita)

We feel comfortable when people around us are of the same colour and belief system. Most of us feel nervous when the 'others' approach us. The thinking then is: 'It is us and them, or us against them. They are not like us, they are different.' We can call this the root cause of all the conflicts. We do not really want to know them. We allow our prejudices and fears to colour our judgements and the distance between us and 'them' widens. Politicians often say that different communities in the United Kingdom are living parallel lives. When we live parallel lives, we can't expect much inner peace as the fear of the 'other' is always gnawing at us.

Seekers of peace will understand that ultimately there is no 'us' and 'them' because everyone is connected. We have to be willing to think at the level of collective consciousness—the awareness that makes us one humanity. We have to challenge the attractions of 'us and them' logic all the time, day in and day out and not allow it to take hold. Connections that are tenuous have to be firmed. It means developing our critical faculty and resisting the temptation to absorb influences which take us away from respecting the 'other.' We talk of inclusiveness, but prefer separateness in real life. The way of peace is at the level of the spirit; it has to come from one's inner self and nowhere else.

STRANGERS

No one is our enemy; no one is a stranger to us. We befriend the whole world. (Guru Granth Sahib)

When we say that 'they' i.e. people we do not like or strangers, are bad, we are implying that we are good. This has been used since times immemorial to justify wars and conflicts. Slogans and denunciations like 'They are evil' can motivate the people to objectify and fight the 'other'. You can justify your criminal behaviour by rationalizing, and defend your actions by making self-statements like 'they deserve what they get'. You have to be responsible for your actions.

We fall back on the eternal distinctions between good and evil. We find somebody to denigrate, make jokes about and attack instead of seeing the enemy within ourselves. If they are creations of the same creator, then we can't really separate ourselves into groups, tribes etc.

When I was new to the North East of England, some people looked at me, smiled and said, "Hello". They must have realized that the "stranger" was like them, with his likes and dislikes, family, friends, problems and so forth. Some people do reach out to strangers first and others ignore them even when they meet the 'known stranger' at the bus stop practically every day. I was grateful when people treated me as a fellow human being. Try reaching out first, and experience the profound feeling of inner happiness.

HATRED

People normally think that it is not possible that hatred can do any harm or one can cultivate hatred till it goes out of bounds. We are civilised people. Let us look at a recent example. On 6th April 1994 a rocket propelled grenade brought down Rwanda's presidential jet, killing the president, Juvenal Habyarimana. Within hours, gangs of young men wielding machetes and an assortment of other weapons were roaming the capital Kigali, hacking to death people from the Tutsi tribe. The killers were from Rwanda's other main ethnic group, the Hutus.

Neighbours turned on neighbours. Priests stood by while members of their congregations were butchered. The hatred turned teachers into child killers. Radio stations controlled by Hutu extremists known as the Interahamwe broadcast orders to kill all Tutsis, whom they called "cockroaches" to be exterminated. The killing only ended when the Rwandan Patriotic Front, led by Paul Kagame, marched from exile in Uganda to seize control of the capital.

When we hate somebody, we hurt ourselves more than the person we hate. Our attention is on him or her, and our personal peace is gone. Hatred arouses other emotions like anger, and unbridled anger can lead to violence. Even if we try to rationalize our actions, feelings and emotions don't change the immorality of violence or any criminal act for that matter.

There is never a "they" who embody total evil, and we can never be totally gentle, kind and understanding. So when feelings of distrust or hatred lead you to some form of action, examine your motives very dispassionately. **Look inward to discover your dark side**.

Fear and suspicion emanate from a lower level of consciousness. Love and sharing emanate from a higher level of consciousness, a Higher Vision of humanity. Most of us operate at a lower level and have a lower vision of humanity. When people are operating at this level, it does not take long to diminish and dehumanise another person, ethnic group or community.

PERCEPTIONS

There is always more than one way of looking at things. You do not have to restrict yourself to look from one angle only.

Life in a complex highly organised society requires considerable trust in others, especially strangers. There is considerable evidence which suggests that 'strangers' are a potent source of fear in the public imagination. Suspicion or perceptions of the 'stranger' can have a corrosive effect because of the fear and anxiety they generate. Self-perceived vulnerability is also crucial to levels of individual fear. A feeling that the neighbourhood is declining and shifts in racial and ethnic numbers seem to be particular sources of fear.

According to de Bono, "perception is a particular of looking at some part of the world. Perceptions are the patterns which form in our minds after exposure to the world at first or second hand. These patterns are only among *some of the many* that could have been formed."[2] If we are stuck with one type of perception, and it is causing inner turmoil, then we should be thinking of new ones and discarding the one which is not serving any useful purpose. You can use different techniques though the aim remains the same—uncovering and changing the concepts and perceptions. Here are some suggested techniques that could help you achieve the aim:

1. Lateral thinking or Creative thinking (new ideas)

2. Brain storming

3. Problem solving.

4. Being benign: A nagging partner could be seen as a loving and caring partner. A stranger could be seen as a source of information or knowledge about a different culture and way of life.

5. Humane impulse: If you are friendly and warm to the stranger, the stranger will react in the same vein.

You can't have personal peace except by relating peacefully. Relationships are the crucible of reality. They test whether you have unconditional regard for the humanity of the other person, if you have discarded layers of distrust and suspicion to relate openly to the other person. The world of fear and suspicion didn't come by accident. You and I experience such a world entirely by choice every day. How you relate will test whether your ideal is actually viable in the rough and tumble of the suspicion-riddled world.

When we trust our views and opinions only and do not give credence to other opinions and perceptions, we get very biased views about each other. This approach can give rise to racial prejudices, sexism, ageism, class identity, feelings of social superiority or inferiority, etc

---

2. de Bono. E. (1977), *Lateral Thinking*, 2nd edition, London.

If you want inner harmony (freedom from inner conflict), you have to be aware of the excuses you make to justify your functioning at a lower level.

Helpful Tips

- We do not have to look for more excuses to be unpleasant or violent to others, but make a conscious decision to be nice to others.

- If you are angry with someone, or hate someone, think about it. Be aware of its characteristic, that it is an impermanent condition. Enemies become friends and friends sometimes start hating the sight of each other.

- Ask yourself: "Is it really necessary? Is there something in it that satisfies you?"

- If it is unnecessary, and nothing in it satisfies you, then get rid of it. It is not your 'self'.

- Move to a Higher Vision of humanity.

INSIGHTFUL MEDITATION

Making peace with oneself

For meditation to be effective, you need to find a time and place which affords you calm and freedom from disturbance. A quiet room with not much in it to distract you would be ideal. For meditation to be effective, the practice must be supported by genuine willingness to investigate and make peace with oneself.

Choose a posture that will keep your back straight. If you are not used to sitting in a cross-legged position on the floor, a simple upright chair may be helpful.

Focus on the breath, and use it as the means of spreading peace and well-being. Visualize the breath as a light, or a warm ray, and let it gradually sweep over your body. (Some people like to focus on a candle or a beautiful flower.) Lightly focus your attention on the chest region around the heart area. Let the awareness of light spread to other parts of the body. Imagine yourself at 'Peace'. Visualizing the breath as having a healing colour could be helpful.

If you were experiencing negative states of mind, on the out-breath, let go of any negativity, stress or worries.

Measuring Your Inner Peace

The exercise on the next page is designed to help you to evaluate your level of Inner Peace. On the Inner Peace Checklist, circle the number that represents where you rate your current level of Inner Peace or Serenity. If you give yourself a low score on a particular item, write down one or two well-considered actions that you can take to focus on what to do about it. For example if you scored low on meaning and purpose in life, you might wish to find meaning for yourself, by your conscience. Meaning must be found and cannot be given. As Frankl says, 'Conscience may be defined as a means to discover meanings to life, to "sniff them" out as it were.'

INNER PEACE CHECKLIST

On a scale of 1 to 10, choose the number that applies to you. 1 is low, and 10 is high.

1. **Inner-directed:** (Guided by own principles, values, etc., rather than by external influences.)
   1, 2, 3, 4, 5, 6, 7, 8, 9, 10

2. **Positive Attitude:** (Avoiding negative thinking, Positive self talk.)
   1, 2, 3, 4, 5, 6, 7, 8, 9, 10.

3. **Stability:** (Can handle stress, mentally and emotionally sound.)
   1, 2, 3, 4, 5, 6, 7, 8, 9, 10

4. **Self-Acceptance:** (Believing in yourself, Being True to yourself.)
   1, 2, 3, 4, 5, 6, 7, 8, 9, 10

5. **Assuming Responsibility:** (Accepting responsibility for your choices.)
   1, 2, 3, 4, 5, 6, 7, 8, 9, 10

6. **Mindfulness:** (Being self-aware. Conscious decision-making.)
   1, 2, 3, 4, 5, 6, 7, 8, 9, 10

7. **Realism:** (Accepting things as they are. Letting go of mistakes.)
   1, 2, 3, 4, 5, 6, 7, 8, 9, 10

8. **Persistence:** (Maintaining the desire to achieve your vision.)
   1, 2, 3, 4, 5, 6, 7, 8, 9, 10

9. **Self-Confidence** (Self-assured. Courage to do what you believe is right.)
   1, 2, 3, 4, 5, 6, 7, 8, 9, 10

10. **Higher Values:** (Commitment to values which will benefit self and the greater whole, or the greater universe.)
    1, 2, 3, 4, 5, 6, 7, 8, 9, 10

11. **Humanity:** (Awareness of the unity of humanity.)
    1, 2, 3, 4, 5, 6, 7, 8, 9, 10

12. **Meaning in life:** (Seeking and fulfilling meaning and purpose of life.)
    1, 2, 3, 4, 5, 6, 7, 8, 9, 10

   - List the items where you scored below—4
   - Think of one or two actions to address the weakest areas.
   - Ask yourself—"How can I develop my realism, so that I do not delude myself and accept things as they are, or how can I improve my self-confidence, or seek and fulfil meaning and the unique purpose of my life?"

Make continence your furnace, and patience your goldsmith
Make understanding your anvil and Divine Knowledge your tools

2

Attachment

For some people, this world is one big amusement arcade, and it is so attractive, so tempting, so inviting, that they are stuck in it, engrossed in it. Such people chase material things from the world and are attached to worldly pleasures.

Normally we say that stingy people are attached to their wealth. They do not enjoy it, but spend all their energy on accumulating it. There are quite a few reports and anecdotes of such people leaving hundreds and thousands of pounds or dollars behind after their departure from this world. Nobody takes a penny or a cent to the other world.

Let me narrate the story of a distant relative of mine who fits into the category. He had quite a few properties around the world, but never carried any money with him when going out with his friends. When asked to pay for a meal, etc., he would say that his wallet was in the other trousers that were at home. When he died, his own children did not know about half of the properties. I assume that the tenants are enjoying the properties at present.

Attachment has nothing to do with experiencing worldly things. It is the mental dependency on them. **Row** offers a good solution when she says, "To remain detached, you do not have to sever relationships or physically remove yourself from a person or object. All you need do is retain your inner independence. When your happiness is not dependent on any object or being, you are not attached to it then."[1]

Ask yourself, 'Are you attached to your nationality, language, race, personal history, habits, car, and money, etc.? You can attract the type of people you want in your life by becoming that type of person. If you want loving people in your life,

---

1.   Row, J. (2007), *The Complete Power,* Mumbai, Vedanta Vision.

you will have to be a loving person first. To acquire this attribute, one needs to be self-aware and changing parts of the personality that do not love. If one wants to live in a world that is less violent, then the individual must become aware of parts of their personality that are violent and do not nurture them. The process of change is not easy, but it is at the heart of spiritual development.

Some people do not change. They remain angry, vengeful, narrow minded, bigoted throughout their lives. They react repeatedly in the same way, because of their psychological and emotional characteristics, and attachment to the same old habits. They create the same experiences and the same consequences again and again, time after time. Other people replace their anger with calmness, with appreciation or lighten up.

When you change yourself and pursue your new values and perceptions, you will no longer be attracted to old friends with the same old habits. When you replace your old habits and characteristics, you will hold the new ones in great esteem, and they will become embedded as well. The attachment to the old ones will gradually dissipate. The process may take time, but you can be what you want to be. Choice is the **power** to make a difference in your life.

We all know that our life is transitory, that we came with nothing and will leave this world with empty hands. Still we place profound value on the acquisition of wealth; I am not saying that we should turn our backs on material possessions. We need money for our subsistence, and we do not have to renounce and live ascetic lives. If we all renounced material things, then we would be mendicants and live on alms only. We have got to be realistic; if we all did that, the world would be a terrible place to live in. There would be no economic, technological or scientific progress in this world and a time might come when there would be nobody to give us any alms when we go begging.

All I am saying is, do not be too attached to them, or be possessed by material considerations. In terms of possessions, we are accumulating so much stuff that there is nowhere to put it all. We buy millions of pounds worth of goods which we never use. Britain alone boasts 3.8 million unused fondue sets. Self-storage facilities are growing every year. We can simplify our lives.

Psychologists have identified four fundamental needs: to feel secure, competent, part of a community, and authentic. On this basis, one can understand people buying things they actually use—futuristic wooden furniture from Ikea, but not why we are blinded by the glare of snazzy gadgets.

Many celebrities seem to have it all but end up in rehabilitation centres. Their inner world is missing.

Perhaps you need to look at yourself to determine whether you are addicted to have more and more? The following questions hopefully will help you in the process:

- Do you express yourself through your material possessions?

- Are you in work that motivates you or in work motivated by greed?

- Do you consider that possessions are as important as people?

- Does your interest in money/materialism prevent you from connecting with your family, friends and the wider community? Are you a workaholic?

- Do you often compare what you own with what others own?

- Do your conversations normally centre on money/materialism or do you enjoy serious discussions and intellectual debates?

If you have answered "yes" to most of the questions, then you have lost the consumer plot. You need to learn how to be detached a little more from material possessions that you are chasing.

Treat each new day as a gift. Anxiousness and envy for what is not, can give way to awareness and gratitude for what is.

NON-ATTACHMENT

Non-attachment is not self-denying. It is life enabling in the sense that it is a win-win situation. As people rise to achieve what is really meaningful to us, they have access to higher aims, their ideals. They are not restricted to the physical plane alone. When people indulge in physical joys alone, the law of diminishing returns kicks in. A time comes when material possessions give no happiness, but our attachment to them does not slacken. But when we listen to our soul or inner core and access our higher values which are intellectually and spiritually fulfilling, physical joys follow.

Attachment implies affection for something or somebody or devotion. John Bowlby in *Attachment and Loss* illustrates the meaning of Attachment well when he says that: "To say of a child that he is attached to, or has an attachment to someone means that he is strongly disposed to seek proximity to and contact with a specific figure and do so in certain situations, notably when he is frightened, tired or ill."

Most child psychologists contend that children become attached to a principal figure who could be a mother, or father and subsidiary figures. Human attachment probably is an instinctive response to the need for protection and survival. We adults become strongly attached to material things also. I am aware that attachment to material things is difficult to give up. We also know that whatever we buy is impermanent, and subject to decay and damage. You may wish to start by reducing your hold on to material attainments in the beginning by reducing your hold slightly so that it becomes a light one. Guru Ramdas (Nanak 4) says: "Holdfast to righteousness and contemplate the Lord's name." So if you want to hold fast on to something, hold fast to virtuous deeds The main aim of life on this earth according to the Sikh Gurus is for the soul to reach complete union with God, to be one with him/her or it.

Some people when preaching about detachment say that "Nothing is mine," which implies that we should throw away all our possessions. In the same vein when somebody says "This is not myself," it can be interpreted as meaning that the person does not value his or her life. My understanding is that both the above statements imply that we should give up attachment to material things. It is not easy, we have to practise loosening our hold, and gain understanding through constant practice. **The real understanding will not come by studying or asking others.** It is something you have to see and know for yourself through practising. Turn inwards to know for yourself instead of looking 'outwards' for answers.

We can argue about attachment, non-attachment and detachment and other philosophical issues at an intellectual level and never really learn anything. Some of us have learnt one approach or another, and we even become attached to the 'approach'. We close our minds to other choices or philosophies and are prepared to defend our 'system' or set of beliefs at any cost, even if it means losing our peace of mind.

Gautama Buddha is regarded as a spiritual guide by his followers. In Four Noble Truths, the first 'Truth' is the recognition of 'dukkha' translated as suffering or un-satisfactoriness. The second Truth is the recognition of what gives rise to suffering, and it is identified as 'tanha—craving for satisfactoriness. It is the attachment to desire,—'I must have it, and it must be mine' mentality.

We create the causes of 'suffering' and it is anxious, restless craving. When I was young, I thought that if I had a pushbike I would be happy. I did not need any other mode of transport. I have got a car now which is in perfect condition and it gets me from A to B, yet I want a better quality car, or a 'more prestigious' one. Craving for material assets never ceases; when we have acquired one, then we want another one advertised on television or the media or the latest model.

Most of us have neither contentment nor calmness of mind because of craving and attachment to material assets. We are never content and hence:

> *Alas! I have neither hope nor health,*
> *Nor peace within nor calm around,*
> *Nor that content surpassing wealth*
> *The sage in meditation found.*
>
> —Stanzas Written in Dejection, near Naples (1818)

"—But nothing is sweeter than to occupy the quiet precincts that are well protected by the teachings of the wise, from where you can look down on others and see them wandering all over the place, getting lost and striving as they seek the way in life, striving by their wits, pitting their noble birth, by night and by day struggling by superior efforts to rise to power at the top and gain possession of all things."—De Rerum Natura bk.2

MATERIAL POSSESSIONS

Those who are contented and at ease when the occasion comes and live in accord with the course of Nature cannot be affected by sorrow or joy. This is what the ancients called release from bondage. Those who cannot release themselves are so because they are bound by material things.—Chuang Tzu

Pursuit of money is considered the greatest good in this age. It affects our culture, our lives and our values.

There is no doubt that we need food to develop and sustain our bodies and water to quench our thirst. Similarly we need clothes to protect us against inclement weather and a roof over our heads. In short, few people can dispute the fact that food, clothes and a house are necessities. Problems arise when we are not satisfied with simple nutritious food but want the best cuisine. Only a mansion will do because of our 'status' in society, and a car is not for transporting us from A to B, but is a symbol of our wealth so it has to be the envy of the whole neighbourhood.

Everyone seems to think that if you get the right house or car, you will be happy. We are all sick from 'Affluenza', a middle-class virus brought on by social and material envy, says Oliver Smith, a psychologist and author of *Affluenza*. The research on human behaviour made him scornful and despairing of the way over-mortgaged, over-aspiring middle-classes shackle themselves to unfulfilling jobs, working excessively long hours and cutting themselves off from proper relationships.

We need to store for the winter and accumulate for the future, but our needs grow continuously, so what we accumulate appears to be inadequate. We never really assess accurately what is needed. Businesses strive to increase their profits, investors want more and shareholders demand bigger dividends. Individuals also want more material things and live in fear of losing what we have.

There may be some people who genuinely do not care for material things, but I still have to come across one. I have heard some sadhus (holy men or ascetics) say that they have denounced money or it is not important to them, but behind the scenes, their relatives, or supporters are more than willing to collect it for them.

Divali or Diwali is the most important Hindu festival which lasts four or five days, the variations depending on the lunar calculations. On the third day, all doors and windows are kept open so that Laksmi (goddess of wealth) may enter the household. The house and its surroundings are illuminated with oil lamps so that Laksmi may see her way clearly. On this day Indian merchants and bankers finalize their account books, and after ending the financial year, offer worship to Laksmi. If we are honest with ourselves, most of us make an obeisance at the altar of wealth every day.

Whether we admit it or not, most of us are obsessed with material things. A story which comes from India goes as follows: The parents of a young man were distressed because he was not taking his responsibilities seriously. A wise man suggested to them that they give him 99 rupees to keep in a safe place. The young man thought hard and decided that it would be better if he had 100 rupees. So he started working and saving. Once he had 100 rupees, he wanted 200 and so on. He was hooked, and a carefree young man was transformed into a person who wanted more and more wealth.

All the known philosophers of the world tell us that money or wealth cannot give us happiness. No doubt money is needed to meet our needs but instead of being in control, we let wealth control us. We become its slaves. We confuse what we want, with what we need. Just like the young man in the above story, we want more and more money, in hundreds first, then in thousands and ultimately to be millionaires. It gives us our identity, our status in society. There is no limit to how much we want, there is no contentment. We define ourselves through our earnings and possessions. We may lose our health, acquire various ailments like high blood pressure, or have heart attacks, but still we do not 'Stop to Think' if we are on the right path. Some studies suggest that a quarter of British people have been mentally sick in the past 12 months and another quarter have been on the verge.

Most of us firmly believe material things and physical comforts to be more important than spiritual values. Oliver James contends that we have become obsessed with measuring ourselves and others through "the distorted lens of affluenza values"—essentially keeping up with the Joneses or with the Patels. We do not seek personal peace but chase and acquire material things every day.

Perhaps there are people who want to lead simple lives, but find it difficult because of fear of what others would say or think about us. The fear is that we will not fit in, will not be appreciated, though the opposite may be true.

Mahatma Gandhi, after much soul searching, decided to lead a very simple life. He wore homespun clothes and kept a goat for his dairy needs. People revered him.

Different texts suggest that Gautma was brought up in a royal household. He lived a life befitting a prince and was shielded from the conditions prevailing outside the palace. On his rare visits outside the palace, Gautama saw an old man, a sick man and a dead man. On his fourth visit in his chariot; he saw an emaciated sash or an ascetic. An ascetic practises severe self-discipline and abstains from all forms of pleasure, especially for religious or spiritual purposes.

Gautama realized that the infirmities of old age and the pain of sickness and death are an inevitable part of suffering of human life and they awaited him as well. He started wondering if there was a way of life that would overcome suffering and lead to tranquillity of mind. Gautama renounced the kingdom, and walked away from his family, the luxuries and stability of the palace. He became a wandering ascetic.

Guru Nanak was approached by a rich man who wanted to acquire more wealth so that his grandchildren and their grandchildren could live in comfort also. His existence centred on making money and nothing else really mattered to him. Guru Nanak gave him a needle and asked him to return it in the next world. The man said that he couldn't take it with him. Guru Nanak asked him: "If you can't take even a needle with you to the next world, then why are you so anxious about acquiring more and more material things?"

In Sanskrit and Indian philosophy, 'Maya' is described as—illusion or the illusionary world of senses. In everyday language, it also means wealth. In Sikhism, the word Maya has been used in two senses, firstly the literal sense of wealth, and secondly in the sense of attractions of wealth and worldly goods. The admonishment is that one should rise above its attractions, as preoccupation with 'maya' is like fire, which is never quenched. It takes a person away from the Reality, and the purpose of one's life on this earth. A person, who advances on the spiritual path becomes detached from its effects.

LIFE IS TRANSIENT

Who ever is born, will pass away,
Every one's turn will come.
(Guru Granth Sahib)

A fakir (ascetic) knocked at the door of a king's palace and said to the sentry on duty, "I want to stay overnight at the inn." (The word inn is used in the historical sense, which means a house providing accommodation for travellers). The sentry barred the fakir from entering the palace, and an argument ensued. The king heard the commotion, and came to the door to enquire.

The king told the fakir that the building was not a guesthouse but his palace. The fakir told the king that he came to the same place about sixty years ago and somebody told him, "This is my palace." The king said that it must have been his grandfather. The fakir said that he came again about twenty years ago, and was informed by someone that it was his palace. The king said that it must have been his father. The fakir asked, "Where are they now?" The king said that they were dead and buried.

The fakir asked: "If this is not an inn where people can rest for some time and move on, then what is it?" The king had a sudden perception of the true position and allowed the fakir to spend the night at the 'inn'.

AUTHENTIC NEEDS/ARTIFICIAL NEEDS

Zukav and Francis say in *The Mind of the Soul*,"Your sense of meaning, like a compass, always points in the direction your soul wants to go. The more closely you follow it, the more meaning you experience, and when you ignore it, the meaning drains from your life." We need to differentiate the authentic needs from the artificial needs. When we follow our deeply held higher values, life is filled with meaning, and when we follow artificial needs, life becomes empty of meaning.

If you want to recognise the difference between your authentic needs and artificial needs, make a list of the things you would like to have and then ask yourself, "is this a need of my soul or a need of my personality?" When I buy new clothes to replenish my wardrobe with clothes which will make me look smarter, it is a need of my personality. When I strive to love others, to serve others selflessly, it is an authentic need which fills my life with meaning.

We all know that our life is transitory, that we came with nothing and will leave this world with empty hands. Still we place profound value on acquisition of wealth. I am not saying that we should turn our backs on material possessions. We need money for our subsistence, and we do not have to renounce everything and live ascetic lives.

All I am saying is—as I said earlier—we do not need be too attached to them, or be possessed by material considerations.

People think that enjoyment lies in the external world and they do everything to entertain themselves with the diverse attractions. The enjoyment which comes is temporary and leaves them with a feeling of emptiness. They forget that it is internal enrichment that makes for true success and fulfilment.

Perhaps you need to look at yourself to determine whether you are addicted to the drug of acquisition—the need to have more and more? Again, the following questions asked earlier will help you:

- Do you express yourself through your material possessions?

- Are you in work that motivates you or in work that is motivated by greed?

- Do you consider that possessions are as important as people?

- Does your interest in money/materialism prevent you from connecting with your family, friends and the wider community? Are you a workaholic?

- Do you often compare what you own with what others own?

- Do your conversations normally centre on money/materialism or do you enjoy serious discussions and intellectual debates?

If you have answered "yes" to most of the questions, then you are probably attached to 'Maya.' You need to learn how to be detached a little more from the material possessions you are chasing.

Treat each new day as a gift. Anxiety and envy for what is not, can give way to awareness and gratitude for what is.

CONSUMERIST LIFESTYLE

The essence of being human is being able to direct your life. The power of choice as far as consumerism is concerned is that you are not overly influenced or persuaded by what the advertisements tell us.

Meet your needs, not your wants, is the old adage. Be yourself and avoid falling into the trap of consumerism. Gadgets keep on appearing on the market, and then within a few months you have a 'newer and a better version.' If you are really directing your life, exercising your choice, you will buy what you need and not what the advertisers want you to have. If you really think hard enough, you will see that you can do without most things. Why go for an iPhone when you have a telephone? If you go back to basics, being grateful for what you have, you won't have to spend long hours to pay for them. The same rule can apply to buying electric goods or cars. Why buy a 4x4 when your small car will transport you from 'A' to 'B' without any hassle?

We get excited about any new gadget that is brought out, whether it is useful or useless is irrelevant. I suppose that we are people who buy things in droves, things we don't need and can't really afford. Affluent consumerist lifestyle is not a western affliction; I think it is worse in developing countries like India as well. Pollution seems to be the number one hazard in Delhi, but still more and more cars are being bought every day.

Before giving in to consumerism, please ask yourself:

1.   Why exactly do I want to have this gadget?

2.   Will not the older/smaller/cheaper thing (which I have) do?

UNBOUNDED CRAVING

We create the causes for our own suffering, the main cause being restless, anxious craving. There are quite a few columnists who write under the heading, 'Shop till you drop', but shop till you drop—or are trampled upon is also a reality. It is not unusual at New Year when major stores put on mega sales. Shoppers crawl, scramble, and clamber over one another to be the first in when the security shutters open. Some even cry when they do not get what they want, i.e. desire not satisfied.

This is where mindfulness comes in. We do not have to be the slaves of unbounded craving. When one becomes a slave of craving, one does all sorts of things that create and nurture suffering. I am not saying that all sorts of desires are wrong; what I am trying to imply is that excessive desire for a certain thing or gadget where you only think about acquiring it, causes suffering.

The desire for food and the normal requisites of life are necessary. When one is hungry and desires food, it is a natural phenomenon. It is a desire within boundaries and does not have ill effects. We need food to be sustained and nourished, and to maintain our health. At a spiritual level, it is also needed to help fulfil the Holy Life.

However, if our life revolves around food only, then it becomes sensuality, it becomes something more than desire. When there is a craving for more and more things to eat, to savour, seeking enjoyment through food and the consumption is unconstrained, that may bring hardship and trouble. This is attachment to food, or the thought of eating delicious food. As it is, we know that obesity is increasing at a very fast rate throughout the world. I know some people who talk of the evening meal while they are having their lunch

Talking about food, we also know that in western countries we waste a lot of food which could feed a whole developing country. This is selfishness, and not mindfulness. A cousin of mine who is really quite well off financially wipes his plate clean before handing it over for cleaning. I have observed him discreetly on a number of occasions, and have never seen even a tiny morsel on his plate after he has finished eating.

The question we need to ask ourselves before buying anything—food or garment—is: Do I really need it?

Through mindfulness, we can aspire to complete freedom from unnecessary suffering.

DOES MONEY BUY HAPPINESS?

It has been folk wisdom that money cannot buy you happiness. Now some experts also agree that money might satisfy some extrinsic needs like status and possession of material goods but does not lead to happiness.

A conference in Brunel University's school of social sciences concluded that subjective factors such as time spent with family tended to have a greater impact on people's sense of well-being than objective factors such as income. It concluded that people tend to place greater emphasis on things that would not bring them happiness. People tend to satisfy their extrinsic desires which include income and status rather than their intrinsic needs such as quality of life and time spent with the family.

Vanuatu, a tiny island in South Pacific, has been voted the happiest place on earth. They don't have money—they use pigs' horns instead!

Some psychologists consider that some rich people spend money in a mad attempt to cover up boredom and depression. For some super rich, houses, yachts and even aeroplanes are like toys, they play with them, lose interest and then buy something else. They are increasingly succumbing to what has been labelled as Wealth Fatigue Syndrome (WFS). Frank James, author of *Richstan,* says that the rich are never happy no matter what they have. They are always comparing themselves with others who have bigger yachts and mansions.

Ordinary people enjoy normal lives; they actually talk with each other and move around freely. The super rich end up with electric gates outside their houses. In some developing countries, they move around with bodyguards or 'gun men' like the Russian oligarch or political leaders in South East Asia.

I DO NOT HAVE A SHIRT

An unhappy king assumed that he would attain happiness if he wore the shirt of a happy man. He sent his minions on a mission to search for a happy person and bring his shirt. The servants searched the whole kingdom but were unable to find a truly happy man. Each person who appeared to be happy was unhappy for one reason or another and had his or her own catalogue of woes. Guru Nanak put it very elegantly when he said: "Nanak, the whole world is suffering."

As they were about to give up their search, they observed a man wearing a loincloth only dancing and singing near a river. When asked if he was really happy, the man replied in the affirmative. The servants told the man that the king would like to wear his shirt to be happy as well. The man danced with joy again and said, "I do not have a shirt."

Top Tip

Lila Das Gupta of England who tried a year without buying anything new says:

"I learnt something we all know, but, in the developed world constantly need reminding of: material goods do make our lives more comfortable, but the best things in life are still free."

3

Values

Rokeach in *The Nature of Human Values* (1973) says that values are a "comprehensive set of standards to guide actions, justifications, judgements, and comparison of self and others." Values aid us to serve needs for adjustment, ego defence and self-actualization.

Values differ from social norms as values are personal and internal. And a social norm is a prescription to behave in a certain situation in a specific way. For example, in the United Kingdom, we used to stand up when the national anthem was played in public places but not when we heard it over the radio or saw it on television at home.

Why have any values? What purposes do they serve?

- Values can be seen as standards that guide ongoing activities.

- Values give expression to human need.

- Values are multifaceted standards that guide our conduct in a variety of ways.

- Values are central to the study of comparisons. We employ them to ascertain whether we are as moral and competent as others.

FUNDAMENTAL CHANGE

It is not unknown for people to change their values completely. In some cases instead of a slight modification to the value system, it may be turned upside down. According to Miller and Banco, people who experienced *Quantum Change* indicated that "everything was different after the change". They were completely transformed.

Their values changed. Their biggest single gain was of the priority given to spirituality which rose from the bottom third to first place for men and third place for women. Both men and women also reflected large increases in the value they placed on forgiveness, generosity, God's will, growth, honesty, humility, loving and personal peace.

Quantum change happened suddenly to people. People changed in a few moments because of a mystical experience or a sudden insight. Usually a mystical experience change includes the experience of being given a message or having an important truth revealed. Perhaps this was Joan of Arc's experience, sometimes caricatured as hallucination or madness. Great religious leaders are reputed have such experiences as well.

Those who experienced the insight suddenly 'came to a new realisation, a new way of thinking or understanding.' The authors say that what seemed to shift was how the person, who had experienced the change, understood and perceived reality. The person's core values changed and became clearer. Here is how a person describes the changes in the priorities:

> *"I am just seeing the brightness in the world, the order of things and how it's supposed to be, as opposed to seeing the discord and disharmony. It's seeing that everything as it should be right now—My motivations and my whole sense of direction in life have changed. My values changed. What I thought was important changed, I just completely shifted gears. It's given me a sense of purpose and direction I never had before, a real meaningful purpose in life"*

Maslow proposes that there are Higher and Lower level values, and also speaks of B (being values) and D (deficiency values). 'Being' is an active vital internal state in which we are able 'to see'. It is obvious that people who experienced the quantum change were transformed in that they adopted Higher-level values.

Some well-known leaders such as Mahatma Gandhi, Martin Luther, and Nelson Mandela often have a 'sense of what it is they are meant to do and must do.'

CODE OF CONDUCT

Rokeach contends that a value refers to a mode of conduct or end state. A value represents a specific preference. A person prefers a mode (instrumental) or end state (terminal value) not only when he or she compares it with the opposite, but also when comparing with other values within his or her value system. The person prefers a particular mode or end state to other modes or end states that are lower down in his or her value hierarchy. Thus people who value contentment as a terminal value, (end state) can have cessation of craving as their instrumental value (mode).

That is why the manner in which a person copes with his problems is the most revealing thing about him. In *Opinions and Personality,* Smith, Bruner and White state that "The solutions to his problems are conserved in the form of values: ways of looking at and evaluating himself, the people about him, and the world around him."

One can infer much about a person by letting him tell what he likes, what moves him and what he is like. That is why the social psychologists—Smith *et al*—contend that the Personality of a person can best be studied by understanding a man's values and philosophy. "Among the most revealing procedure used in our procedure (exploration of ten adult men—men very much in the midst of life) was a two-hour interview on **Personal Values and Religious Sentiments**, which began with a question on: **What things really matter to you most in life?—and moved widely over the philosophy of life.**"

CHANGE

When spiralling downward into desperation, people quite often turn for help to something greater and wiser than themselves.

Life can be transformed. It can be a sweeping and permanent transformation, if you are true to your guiding principles

People who are unhappy or discontented often say that "nothing can be done about my life—I am at breaking point. The burden is becoming unbearable."

Life can be transformed if you were to understand your values well. It may be beyond your imagination right now, but sweeping and permanent transformation is possible. You have to work slowly at it. It is possible that you have the wrong priorities; the things which are really important are obscure or have not been given due prominence. It is not unusual for people to change their priorities; the ones which were peripheral at one time, at some stage become central. Some realize that as kids, they were formed into something that was not their natural self. They realize with maturity that what is in their minds is distorted. This type of insight might involve the whole person—thoughts, actions, emotions and spirit.

The insight may in some ways represent a change in the personal sense of self. Sometimes it is a simple decision, a logical, wilful process that includes analysis and assessment. People weigh up the pros and cons, and come to the rational conclusion that change is needed. That sets the process of change in motion—to be what they could be rather than stay as they are.

When you consciously prioritise your values, you are looking at the picture through a different lens, and we can view life through a variety of lenses.

FREE AGENTS

In Psychology there is always a debate as to whether we are determining or determined. Let us think of animals first of all to elucidate this point. A lion will starve but will not eat grass. A cow on the other hand will die rather than eat meat. Farmers in England learnt the harsh lesson when they mixed minced meat with their fodder. The cows got BSE and about 250,000 had to be culled. Human beings are free to eat what they like.

Let us take another example. If a lion kills a human being, it cannot be charged with murder in a court of law. If a herd of cows enter a farmer's field and eat or destroy the crop, the herd cannot be charged with Theft, Criminal damage, or a Conspiracy to Damage Property. If human actions are included in the deterministic system, it would follow that no one could have ever acted otherwise than he or she did—and therefore human beings are not morally responsible for their actions.

We can act the way we like, choose our priorities; in short, we are free agents and have free will. When we act in one way, we are aware that we could have acted otherwise. However, it is worth mentioning here that the philosopher, John Stuart Mill, has questioned if we have such awareness. He has argued that we have always acted on our strongest motivation.

As far as the search for personal peace or inner tranquillity is concerned, both the propositions can serve our purpose. When we prioritise our values, we increase our motivation. The act of prioritising by itself is a big motivator. So if you attempt the following exercise, you will become more aware as to what is really important to you. Just as it can be predicted that somebody who values intellectual and logical qualities may become a professor or an academic one day, so there is a likelihood that a person who values inner peace will strive to attain personal tranquillity or equanimity.

HELPFUL SUGGESTIONS

• Take responsibility for your life and do not be a slave of your past. You do not have to be a victim of your history.

• Have a sense of yourself as a person of profound calmness—nicer, sweeter and happier.

YOUR VALUES (What is most important)

Following are some Values in an alphabetical order. From the list, identify the top ten which are most important to you. Place 1 (one) next to the value which is most important and 2 next to the value which is second most important, and so on.

1. Acceptance—to be accepted as I am

2. Ambitious—hard working, aspiring

3. Broadminded—tolerant, open minded

4. Capable—competent, effective

5. Caring—kind, humane

6. Comfortable life—to have a pleasant enjoyable life

7. Contribution—to give money or help to a common cause

8. Compassionate—merciful, willing to alleviate suffering.

9. Courageous—standing up for your rights

10. Ecological—to live in harmony with the environment

11. Faithful—logical, trustworthy

12. Famous—well known, socially recognised.

13. God's will—to seek and obey God's will

14. Growth—to keep changing and growing

15. Happiness—contentedness

16. Healthy—to be physically well

17. Helpful—giving help, being useful

18. Honest—sincere, truthful

19. Independent—self reliant, free from dependency

20. Inner peace—personal peace

21. Intellectual—intelligent, reflective

22. Logical—rational

23. Loving—affectionate

24. Moral—concerned with the distinction between right and wrong

25. Obedient—dutiful.

26. Peace—tranquil life. Peace in the world.

27. Power—to have control over others

28. Responsible—dependable, reliable

29. Self-controlled—self-disciplined

30. Service—to be of service to others

31. Tolerance—to accept and respect those different from me.

32. Truth—being truthful.

33. Virtue—to live a morally pure life

34. Wealth—Plenty of money

35. Wisdom—to have a mature understanding of life

After you have ranked the values and prioritised the **TEN** most important to you, please answer the following questions:

1. How do you feel about the way you have ranked the values? (on a scale of 1 to 10 write the number which describes how you feel—10 signifies that you do care much about the order in which you ranked the values, and 1 (one) tells you that you do not care much about the order in which you ranked the values. Or—Do you feel that your ranking was a bit haphazard and you did not give it much thought. Did you do the ranking conscientiously?

2. How satisfied do you feel about the way you have ranked the values?

3. Which rankings do you feel satisfied or dissatisfied with?

4. Do you find the exercise thought provoking?

5. Do you think it will lead you to do some more thinking about your values?

6. How would a person who really values personal peace, and retains equanimity whatever the circumstances rank the same values?

We shall revisit this Values exercise once again, so please keep the rankings in a safe place.

CHANGE IN VALUES

There are therapists out there but the real impetus for value change will come from you. When you did the values exercise, you, my esteemed reader, examined what is really important to you. This book aims to set the conditions for a learning experience to take place. Your values, and what things are really important to you are matters which deserve most serious consideration, not only now but through out your life. That is why you are being asked to do the Values exercise once again after reading the whole book.

Once you are aware of your values, your regard for the most important will increase significantly. It is possible that you place a high premium on *inner peace* because you are not satisfied with your current lifestyle. You are seeking meaning to your life. It is also possible that your life at present is dominated by conflicts, anxieties, competitive behaviour, and difficulties in interpersonal relations.

It is not unusual for people to feel dissatisfied with themselves. Human beings have been seen as capable of feeling satisfied or dissatisfied with themselves as they become aware of discrepancies that involve their self-conception. At this point, you may want to ask yourself: If you are not satisfied with some aspects of your life, what are you doing about it?

If you really value *inner peace* and the related values, you are likely to focus attention on the target value/s. The focus will depend upon the degree of dissatisfaction you have with your self-concept and the value—in this case *inner peace*. Your efforts will be directed towards harmonising your self-concept and the value.

Those of you who have seen '**You Are What You Eat**' documentaries on television might have observed the fundamental changes which take place in the participants. It becomes obvious that before their participation in the programme, 'Health' or 'Fitness' was not given much importance. But after realizing the damage they were doing to their bodies, most of the participants change their lifestyles. Some pick up a bar of chocolate in a store, but after some reflection return it to the shelf. Initially, what they eat is prescribed by the 'trainer', but gradually the participants take responsibility for what they eat.

There is a saying that there is a slim person hidden in every fat person waiting to come out. The slim person will manifest if people are sufficiently motivated to make it possible. Maslow refers to self-actualisation as a need and a high order value.

VALUES AND BEHAVIOUR

Values are significantly related to all kinds of attitudes, and values are also strongly related to behaviour. So when the participants in 'You are What You Eat' become conscious of the conflict between self-concept and their value system, i.e. slim and healthy—as opposed to what they actually are—obese and unhealthy, their priorities change. They put their new belief system into action by buying healthier food and exercising more. The 'I' changed which said: 'I am not satisfied with myself.' This is what I am now, but not what I want to be or could be—the level at which an event creates the discordance, affects the breadth and permanence of change. The more central the level at which a change occurs, the more enduring and far reaching its effects are likely to be. The programme does not try to change the behaviour only by saying eat this food or do this and that.

'What You Eat is What You Are' creates an inner conflict from a clashing of 'how I am' and 'how I want to be'. The programme facilitates the awareness by talking about different types of food or lifestyles and what they do to you. The dissatisfaction comes from within. The programme only promotes the discovery process; the dissatisfaction was probably already present in the participants. It was repressed or not given much prominence in the conscious mind.

Just like any session with a competent therapist, or professional, there is a bit of confrontation in the initial stages, which is inevitable, but the participants are not forced to give in, or concede a point. The confrontation is gentle, and evidence is presented to support assertions made by the 'trainer.'

I have come across quite a few clients who have come through 'cold turkey' and given up misusing illicit drugs. I must admit that not every one succeeded, but they tried especially when they realized the harm they were doing to themselves and their families. Their minds were on feeding their addiction only. Other things were secondary to them.

Some sought help from specialist agencies, and one or two even decided that they had a better chance of overcoming the addiction in residential settings. A person who succeeded by doing cold turkey described his experience as follows: "I could not clothe my children; I could not feed my family because of my dependency on cocaine. I decided to give up the habit, because I could not bear my family suffering any longer. I locked myself in a room, suffered the tremors, sweated like a pig, and bore all the withdrawal symptoms and associated discomfort. I am still clean and happy because I value my family's happiness."

When people have a goal, their life revolves around that aim. They think and breathe that aim and they consider different options to achieve that dream. With determination and tenacity, they do succeed.

SELF-CONCEPT

Self is the 'I' that thinks, feels and acts. If asked to explain the 'components' that make up this self, they would probably include your body, your 'personality', that is, the way you behave.

Our thoughts, perceptions and feelings change very frequently. According to Carter in *Consciousness,* "Even if you take the sum of your experience, your personal history, you will find it is not written in stone. Memories change. The story is constantly being edited and elaborated."

The essential "I" is so fundamental that it is impossible to imagine it away. One can strip away the 'public aspects of self', erase the familiar 'contents' of your mind, and still there is the sense of being "I", a 'subject ground' of self on which all the rest is built. Rokeach's explanation is "the most central of all levels in a personality is the individual's sense of self. This includes as well as the experienced core of identity that persists through out life—the deepest part of oneself that is the same across all the years." For Carter "It is a set of concepts—intuitive unconscious beliefs and ways of interpreting information …"

So when somebody says "I changed", it suggests involvement all the way to the level of self-conception. From some perspectives, it might be called the soul or spirit of the person. If the self is the essence of the person, the core of the person, a change in self-conception should lead to changes in terminal values, in instrumental values, and in functionally related attitudes and behaviour. The person who says "I changed" probably had experienced a high level of self-dissatisfaction prior to the fundamental change or major transformation.

The following questions could help you to decide if you are leading a life consistent with your **Values.**

• What is it that you value and hold dear?

• What things do you strive for most in your life?

• Is your current behaviour consistent with your roles and goals that are important to you?

EMBODYING THE VALUES

If you have a problem identifying your highest Values, think about the characteristics you have or would like to cultivate as a person, a professional, a father/mother, leader, team player and be a role model for others. Ask yourself:

* How do I want to live in this world?

* What values will make my life more fulfilling or meaningful?

All the values listed, like caring, compassion, faithful, growth, honesty, loving, peace, responsible, trust, truth, wisdom etc., are worthy of embodying and pursuing. It is for you to choose the ones that are very pertinent to you. It means that you have to take stock of yourself, what you believe in, and what kind of world you want to create for yourself, for your family, friends and even your community. Even though you are one person, your actions, thoughts and beliefs can make a difference to your network. The ripple effect will cascade to others. If you do well in life, at your work or in sports, your family and friends are happy for you. If you live a principled life, some will try to emulate you. It is the many "I's" that make up the "we."

You can decide to change your home or environment into a more peaceful and loving place for your children to inherit. It is your learning, practising and modelling of fairness, justice, kindness, love, spirituality, truth and wisdom that teach your children the same values.

Take a few minutes to identify your values, the ones that are most important to you. The purpose of finding your values is so that you can endeavour to practise and embody them in your life. Use the 'My Highest Values' exercise to go about cultivating them in yourself so that they serve you to have a meaningful and fulfilling life.

MY HIGHEST VALUES

The purpose of finding your values is so that you do not forget them but consciously practise and embody them in your life.

1. My most important value is:
    The actions I can take to live this value in my personal life are
    A.

B.

C.

The actions I can take to live this value in my work life, business life or in my professional life are:

A.

B.

C.

2. My second most important value is:
    The actions I can take to live this value in my personal life are:
    A.
    B.
    C.

    The actions I can take to live this value in my work life, business life or in my professional life are:

3. My third most important value is:
    The actions I can take to live this value in my personal life are:
    A.
    B.
    C.

    The actions I can take to live this value in my work life, business life, or in my professional life are:
    A.
    B.
    C.

4. My fourth most important value is:
    The actions I can take to live this value in my personal life are:
    A.
    B.
    C.

    The actions I can take to live this value in my work life, business life or in my professional life are:
    A.

B.

C.

5. My fifth most important value is:
    The actions I can take to live this value in my personal life are:
    A.
    B.
    C.

    The actions I can take to live this value in my work life, business life or in my professional life are:
    A.
    B.
    C.

DISSATISFACTION

It is possible that you have a mentor or a friend or even a therapist to assist you to resolve your personal difficulties, but the real impetus for value change ultimately comes from you. My aim in this book is to set the conditions for a learning experience to take place. So let me reiterate that your values and what things are really important to you are matters which deserve most consideration, not only now, but throughout your life.

Once you have completed the values exercise, and done it conscientiously, your regard for your top ranking values will increase significantly. You can use scientific knowledge to know what instrumental values or skills are needed to achieve your terminal values. Roger explains this point clearly when he says if he valued knowledge of "three R's", as a goal of education, scientific methods can provide him with the necessary knowledge. If problem-solving ability was a goal of his education, the scientific method can provide him with the same kind of help. "I may value college success. Then I can determine whether problem solving ability or knowledge of the three R's is most closely associated with that value. I may value personal integration or vocational success or responsible citizenship. I can determine whether problem-solving ability or knowledge of the three R's is better for achieving any one of these values."

So if you value *inner peace*, you need to determine whether confidence, or honesty, or release from long standing negative emotions, or a sense of who you are and who you are not or deeper spirituality is better for achieving your goal. You may want to develop all of the said traits to achieve your cherished value.

It is possible that *inner peace* or serenity is very high up amongst your values because you are not satisfied with your current lifestyle. You are seeking a meaningful life and maturity, or another explanation could be that your lifestyle is dominated by conflicts, anxieties, compulsive behaviour, and difficulties in interpersonal relations.

It is not unusual for people to feel dissatisfied with themselves. Human beings have been seen as capable of feeling satisfied or dissatisfied with themselves as they become aware of discrepancies that involve their self-conception. According to Rokeach, self-dissatisfaction arises when there is a contradiction with self-conceptions and change is motivated by the desire at least to maintain and if possible to enhance conceptions of oneself as a moral and competent human being. "It is easy to see how one's conception may be maintained or enhanced by increasing one's regard for such values as *equality, freedom, and a world of beauty* or by decreasing one's regard for such values as *a comfortable life, national security—*."

However, contradictions with self-concepts do not necessarily mean that change will follow. Some people say that they believe in a certain value, but their actions are not congruent with their values. People who said that they valued altruism ignored a bystander in trouble in some studies. You may wish to ask yourself if you demonstrate the top ten ranked values in your life. If you do not demonstrate them, how could you do so in different aspects of your life?

Commitment to the professed values is crucial, and actions need to be in congruence with the values. Gardeners prepare the seedbed before sowing seeds, and then they water and feed them with the necessary nutrients. The seeds germinate almost immediately, and develop into plants or trees. It is also a fact that a split seed will not grow, it has to be complete, or whole. Similarly if you are double-minded, doubting yourself, then it is difficult for the traits or target values to be embedded.

Attention has to be focused on the target value, increasing its importance to you. The importance will probably hinge on the level of dissatisfaction people have with the self-concept and the target value or values.

Questions which you need to ask yourself are:

- If you really value inner harmony, what are you doing about it?

- What four things are you prepared to do to show your commitment to the target value or values?

SOME HELPFUL SUGGESTIONS

- Meet each day by itself because there is going to be something new each day that we can learn from.

- Forget yesterday's quarrels because you are starting afresh when meeting a new day.

- See more beauty in the world.

- Don't sweat the small stuff.

- Try not to get mad, or stomp off when things are not working your way. See the positive side of everything. If things are not working your way, explore how you can change the situation.

- You do not have to scurry all over to achieve results. Have a plan instead.

- Accept that there are certain things that are beyond our control.

DO WHAT YOU OUGHT TO DO

According to some thinkers there are three types of people in this world, the inactive, the active—who craves for worldly possessions—and the principled.

The inactive person lacks motivation and could be indifferent because there is no goal, no objective to strive for.

Then we have the second type of people who are driven to incessant activity because they are chasing material possessions. Such people have myopic vision, and their mind may not be at ease. Their mind could be in turmoil because after acquiring 50,000 dollars or pounds they want 100,000 and then one million. They want a bigger bank balance, a bigger house and so on. 'How to make money' books sell well in the bookshops.

The third type of person has higher values, a noble vision, and is deeply inspired to act. Such a person is calm, the thinking is clear because he or she is self-aware, and the actions are based on a clear vision. The actions are service oriented rather than self-centred. Such a person finds fulfilment in the performance of any task, and is unconcerned with awards or fruit of action. Such people concentrate on doing the job to the best of their ability. They are aware that the result will come—it has to come. The difference is that they do not crave for the fruit of action and in the process make their lives miserable.

THE RIGHT GOAL

If one does not have any high values, then obviously, the goal cannot be value based, or really important in life. Some of us think of a goal midway and do not succeed. Once you have set yourself a goal, one based on what is really important to you, a higher self-ideal, then you can work out a plan of action to achieve it. We do not have to worry whether we will fail or succeed in reaching our goal, but instead invest in the action that ensures success. It is a process and not an event.

It becomes a mission in life. To realize the goal, the thoughts, emotions and actions are directed towards it.

4

Strong And Secure

To make ourselves strong and secure from harm, said Epicurus, we need to get a clear understanding of four matters—God, death, pleasure and suffering. All our fears and desires are comprehended in these four subjects, so to grasp the truth about them will free us and give peace of mind.

GOD

Most of us take God in some superficial way in order to take care of our needs for power or something like that.

Epicurus's view of a deity is that it is a blessed one and tranquil being. A deity is not actuated by anger or favour, nor possessed by any interest in imposing requirements of any kind on us. From such a being, we have nothing to fear. We can instead treat the idea of such a deity as a model for us to emulate; its peacefulness, detachment, and unending pleasure are exactly what we should seek to achieve in our lives.

God as described by Guru Nanak in the Divine Hymn is:

God is one; His/Her name is True. He/She is Ever existing, Fearless, Inimical to none, Unborn, Deathless, Self-existent, Self-illuminated, and ever true. He/She is the Creator of all that is seen or unseen. He/She will live forever.

Note: Guru Granth Sahib—the Holy Scripture is gender neutral

There is always a debate going on as to whether God exists or not. With some of us, it is a hypothesis, an intellectual exercise, reasoning whether there is a God. I do not wish to indulge in the debate to justify the existence of God, except to acknowledge that my belief in God is heavily influenced by my religion—which is Sikhism.

We operate inside of this funny little human mind that we have, that is too small to comprehend that God is so large, and so all pervasive. God is us. God is outside of us and inside of us and through us, all around us. God is the Great Spirit, out there somewhere, but you can feel the spirit within you. The devotees of God have a sense of the sacred and of responsibility not only for themselves, but for others and the world around them. A Sikh Ardas (Supplication) is never complete without seeking the welfare of all—May all prosper according to Your Will.

Jap sahib composed by the tenth Guru, Guru Gobind Singh, is a long hymn which tells us that there is only One God—Who has been existing since ages and Who will continue to exist forever. He/She has no colour, caste or form, etc., and is above all the gods and goddesses. He is self illuminated and has been called by countless Names (many of which are given in this Hymn); these Names denote the qualities, glories and excellences of God, Who is Merciful, Immortal, Bodiless, and Indestructible. There are about 732 different names for the Almighty.

God has no marks, no colour, no caste, or lineage
None can describe His form, complexion, outline and costume.

God is present in all and His grandeur will never vanish
Salutations to God, Who is Invincible, Who has no particular name and
Who lives in all living beings.
God is the Primal Soul

All souls originate from God's Soul.
God is One, yet He can be seen in innumerable creations created by Him

—(Guru Gobind Singh)

A true believer in God hates the idea of distinction between human beings on the basis of caste, class, religion, creed, nationality, etc. Such a person loves all as 'children of God.'

All men are the same though they appear different
The bright and the dark, the ugly and the beautiful,

The Hindus and the Muslims have developed in accordance with their dif-
ferent surroundings;
All human beings have the same eyes, the same ears,
The same body build composed of earth, air, fire and water.

—(Guru Gobind Singh)

DIFFERENT NAMES—SAME GOD

Allah is simply the Arabic for God, just as Waheguru (Wondrous Lord) is for the Sikhs. God is in English, just as God is Deus in Latin and Bog in Russian. The Koran has 99 names for God; Guru Granth sahib has innumerable names for God as well.

Karta (The Creator) and **Karim** (The beneficent) are the names of the same God.
Razak (The provider) and **Rahim** (The merciful) are also the names given to him.

Let no man in his error wrangle over differences in names.
Worship the One God who is Lord of all.
Know that his form is one and He is the one Light diffused in all.

—(Guru Gobind Singh)

ETHICAL LIVING

Jerry Lynch in his inspiring book *Creative Coaching* says that the head coach of the University of Iowa women's team has one rule: **Do the right thing**. "This clever directive covers a myriad of situations and makes the global assumption that her athletes are reasonable, mature and wise enough to know right from wrong in most situations."

The origin of medical ethics can be traced back to the 4th century B.C. They encompass the Hippocratic writings, contributions made by religious works, liberal theorists, and moral theologians. What emerged was a framework underpinned by core values within which to understand ethical dilemmas. Some ethical practices may change over time, like at present abortion at 23 weeks time is considered to be ethically acceptable because according to some in the medical profession the foetus cannot survive outside the womb at this stage. The thinking may change in the future. But two of the lasting concepts still are: First, do no harm. The second is beneficence, which implies that a doctor should always act in the best interests of the patient.

The American Declaration of Independence which is embedded in the consciousness of every school child in the United Sates says: 'We hold these truths to be self evident, that all men are created equal, that they are endowed by the Creator with certain inalienable rights, that among these are Life, Liberty and the pursuit of Happiness.'

There are some people who treat us well and there are others who treat us badly, it all depends on circumstances, conditions, and our relationship with them. What the others do is up to them, but you can change your attitude to others. You can take moral responsibility for your actions, be kind, cooperative and compassionate, to keep your equilibrium and tranquillity, or be nasty to others and lose your peace of mind.

Some writers take the view that the teachings of Confucius are characterized by the central value of benevolence. Benevolence is characterized by interconnectedness. I also feel that the major religions are also illustrative of the concept of benevolence. I acknowledge that sometimes violence is committed in the name of God—many have been wounded in conflicts initiated by fanatics, but religion should not be a vehicle of hatred. We need to understand their essence, to appreciate that they are demonstrative of the value of benevolence.

Most of us firmly believe that, "I am the best judge of what is right or wrong," though we do not have a firm guide to good conduct. We have man-made laws, some of them probing deep into our lives. But when we use tools like Anti Social Behaviour Orders (ASBOs), they fail to tackle incivilities and bad behaviour because individuals abdicate personal responsibility. Secularists will dismiss this as absurd, but the well known religions of the world taught us a great deal about moral conduct and moral values which laid a solid moral foundation.

In this modern age, everybody has to make their own rules that work for them, but we have also to remember that the personal rules will affect others as well. When we make a rule for ourselves, or behave in a certain way, it has a ripple effect in society. We want a 'responsible society' and not an irresponsible one, a civilised society and not a condition where incivility prevails. When we consider the well-being of others when making decisions, then the decisions will be ethical ones, and you will be cultivating an ethical nature. We are more concerned about the ripple effect that your decisions and actions are going to have, because we realise how interconnected all of us are. You no longer think of yourself as an isolated person.

The late W.F Deeds noted in one of his 'Notebooks' in a newspaper that in the past "children grew up with a more clear sense of what is right and what is wrong than some have now. This went into decline. Thinking underwent a change in the 1960's when religion was seen by some as an obstacle to some of life's pleasures such as promiscuous sex."

If we do not have a deeply held faith, but are fully aware of our values, and they are higher values, they can be our guide to good conduct. They can be the lighthouse which guides us through life; otherwise we are lost in the wilderness without a map. Without higher values, we can have the wrong map which again leads us nowhere.

MORAL COMPASS

In this modern age there are as many moralities as holders of them. Some of us have a strong grounding in what is right and wrong, what is fair and what is unfair and others are not tuned in to their inner voice. Sometimes we say that so and so doesn't have a conscience. My experience in the probation service tells me that most of the offenders have a conscience, but it is suppressed. I have come across quite a few offenders who had a good insight into what they were doing, knew that it was wrong, but then their needs overrode their inner voice. If they had a dependency on illicit drugs or alcohol, then all they thought about most was about the next fix or the next bottle.

Because of different demands and pressures, we rarely have time to develop a realistic sense of our moral and spiritual ideas. Our morality is quite often surface morality only. We rarely have time to consider the importance of the rights of others and our responsibilities and develop a sense of conscience.

If one is not mindful, one thought can lead us astray as when your immune system is not strong and one bacterium can cause infection. Our inner voice, our soul, is our moral compass. The conscience always points towards higher values, like Truth, Honesty, Integrity, Justice etc. The only problem is that we do not have time to go into our souls. We are busy fulfilling our desires, our appetites and the inner voice gets drowned.

Just as a boat will reach the harbour because the captain follows the right course, you will also reach your destination if you conscientiously follow your conscience. **Peace** comes when you dedicatedly follow your course.

COURAGE

Fortune favours the brave in real life is an old saying. Cowardice, pusillanimity and weakness in the face of adversity are bedfellows of failure. So it is important to distinguish between various types of courage.

- **Moral courage**: Moral courage is perhaps the most difficult type in our lives. It is knowing what is right and wrong and not resorting to telling half-truths or fudging. It is the courage to do the right thing especially in difficult circumstances. It is the ability to be honest in the face of adversity.

- **Interpersonal courage:** It involves being honest with other people and being upfront with them. It is the courage to deliver difficult messages. Ever tried to let people who are not nice to others or oppressive know that their behaviour is below par? It is the willingness and ability to challenge others assertively and constructively when confrontation is needed. It means standing up to bullies when necessary. It is easier to back down or back away from these individuals rather than confront them. But if you do not confront them, they grow and others join them.

- **Risk taking**: Some people are too cautious to succeed. They fear failure, and commit insufficient energy to succeed. Sometimes at our work places and outside work, we have to act on imperfect information, but carefully weighed.

- **Physical courage**: We normally associate physical courage with battlefields and warriors. Honours are awarded to the brave for some courageous acts, as they are an example and inspiration to others. But in everyday lives, physical courage is also about endurance and pushing yourself to achieve whatever goals you have set for yourself.

Most of us have one aspect of courage or another, but imagine how you will feel if you develop and integrate all the four facets.

INTELLIGENCE QUOTIENT, EMOTIONAL INTELLIGENCE, SPIRITUAL INTELLIGENCE

Mental Intelligence

Humans have a range of different abilities. Intelligence can be equated with how high or low a person scores on a particular ability scale. For example Intelligence Quotient (IQ) tests reflect verbal and reasoning ability.

The problem with mental intelligence tests is that they do not necessarily give due weight to other aspects of intelligence that are important as well, There is great deal more to everyday living than what the intelligence tests measure. The tests fail to take into account such important facts as motivation, social skills, persistence in the face of adversity, and ability to set and achieve reasonable goals. IQ tests ignore interpersonal skills such as understanding other peoples' states of mind or knowing how to put people at ease.

Intelligence tests were used and are still used for selection—whenever the number of candidates exceeds the number of places—whether in industry or education or the public sector. Psychologists also use them for vocational guidance. They advise individuals as to what kind of job is likely to give them most satisfaction and to make the best use of their talents. In the last decade, the emphasis shifted to emotional intelligence mainly due to the works of people like Daniel Goleman, Richard Boyatiz, Anne McKee, Stephen Fry and others. Their assertion is that being smart is not enough to get on a path of excellence but knowing how we handle ourselves and others is.

Emotional Intelligence

Emotional intelligence refers to the capacity for recognising our feelings and those of others, for managing well our own emotions and of being sensitive to those we are interacting with. The theory has been credited to the US academics John Mayer and Peter Salovey although Daniel Goleman is one of the best-known authors on the subject. Mayer defines emotional intelligence as: *The ability to perceive, to integrate, to understand and reflectively manage one's own and other people's feelings.*

Research shows that in the long run, emotional intelligence is a more accurate determinant of successful communications, relationships and leadership than mental intelligence. In fact Goleman advances the view that emotional intelligence matters twice as much as cognitive abilities such as IQ or technical expertise. The brain may come in useful as may social class and luck, but EQ was the real predictor of who will succeed in an area of life.

Daniel Goleman in *Working with Emotional Intelligence* says that we need to develop five competencies of emotional intelligence for outstanding performance. In his Emotional Competence Framework he divides the five dimensions of emotional intelligence into Personal Competence and Social Competence (pp. 26, 27). The three personal competencies determine how we manage ourselves. They are: Self-Awareness (knowing one's internal states, preferences, resources and intuitions), Self-Regulation (managing one's internal states, impulses and resources), and Motivation (Emotional tendencies that guide or facilitate reaching goals). The social competencies determine how we handle relationships and they are Empathy (awareness of others' feelings, needs, and concerns), and social skills (Adeptness at inducing desirable responses in others).

SPIRITUAL INTELLIGENCE

The whole objective of the human being is to free the personality from the contraction of self in desire into the expression of soul in love. (Rabindranath Tagore)

To live well is to have an ordered soul, one which is in harmony with itself.

When I retreat into the inner sanctuary of the soul, I enjoy the tranquil flow of loving thoughts passing through my being.

The Oxford Dictionary describes the soul as: The principle of life actions in man, commonly regarded as an entity distinct from the body; the spiritual part of man in contrast to the purely physical.

In a survey of 735 managers by the Roffery Park Institute, the study found that 70 per cent were looking for a greater sense of meaning or purpose in their lives. Meaning was seen as connecting with others, having a sense of personal purpose, a heightened sense of what is **really important**, what it is really to be human.

Talk about spirituality, and people come up with different definitions. Some state that they are not religious, but spirituality is important to them. For them, spirituality is listening to beautiful music or witnessing the beauty and harmony of nature.

Some take the extreme or stereotypical view and relate it to monks, sadhus and fakirs (holy men) who live in contemplation and have little connection with the everyday world. Some Indians live in thrall of these sadhus and fakirs and tend to revere them. I am a bit sceptical of these 'holy men' and consider that the majority of them are fake, charlatans who will take your money at the earliest opportunity. Anyway, nowadays it is not just an eastern view that values the individuals who cultivate their inner spiritual life, but a universal view.

Guru Nanak—the founder of Sikhism—when asked to wear a sacred thread made out of cotton (jneu) according to the Hindu custom declined to wear it and said that he wanted a sacred thread that will never break or become old or be destroyed. He highlighted the following virtues which will never be destroyed:

Out of the cotton of **compassion**
Spin the thread of **contentment;**
Tie the knot of **continence,**
Give it the twist of **truthfulness,**
Make such a sacred thread
O Pundit (priest) for **inner self**
Such a tread will not break
Nor get soiled, be burnt, or lost;
Blessed is the man, O Nanak
Who makes it a **part of his life** …

Guru Nanak's truthfulness means a self-respecting people who live in deep harmony with each other, human relationships based on equality, faith in one GOD and brotherhood/sisterhood of all.

Some people may not call it spiritual practice, but they believe that helping others is their highest goal. **I slept and dreamt that life was joy. I awoke and saw that it was service. I acted, and behold, service was joy.** (Rabindranath Tagore.)

The Dalai Lama, in *The Art of Happiness at Work,* says that he finds the use of analytical meditation helpful to generate deeper conviction in the principles of non-violence, of compassion, of forgiveness, especially toward the Communist

Chinese. He thinks that his political work influences his spiritual practice, "my understanding of how my work in relation to the issue of Tibet is in actual fact part of my life-long daily spiritual practice, the practice of someone who deeply believes that helping others is the highest goal of a spiritual practitioner."

For some people, spirituality is transpersonal, and they seek 'a path to oneness with something greater than we'. Victor Frankl's spiritual freedom was one thing that couldn't be taken away from him. It was what made life meaningful and purposeful. Frankl in *Man's Search for Ultimate Meaning* (2000), talks of "another dimension, a world beyond man's world" which probably equates to religion.

Scientists and craftsmen have moulded things so that they meet our needs. Machinery has been made from different metals and ornaments from silver gold, etc. we have utensils to cook and store food. All these things are for our physical comfort and survival. We become attached to material possessions because of the physical comfort derived from them.

The needs of the spirit are different from the requirements of the physical body. Security, shelter and sustenance are the basic needs of the body. We acquire riches to feel more secure, but quite often lose our inner peace. The spirit requires higher goals or ideals. Once we are conscious of our values, what is meaningful, or have a vision, the intellect can be used to achieve the end goal. When we have an elevated vision, our mind is relaxed. Just like we have invented and crafted different materials to be congruent to our needs, the values need to be congruent with the needs of the soul.

Spiritual intelligence is I suppose following what your spirit wants you to do so that your life is driven by a divine conscience. Spiritual intelligence is being true to your highest values. You lose yourself in the service of others, doing well by doing what your inner voice tells you is good. You do not talk only of high ideals, and values, but provide a living example. Every choice you make provides you an opportunity to grow spiritually, to learn what has meaning for you, and what is meaningless, what gives you inner peace and what creates painful experiences.

It is not a world denying ascetic withdrawal, but an active participation to render **useful service**. Once you are aware of your destiny, your calling, then the 'why' about your existence, the search for meaning/purpose in life will be overshadowed by the 'how'?

Your commitment to your deeply held ideals and putting them into practice will have an impact on your attitude to life. In turn, your work and your conduct which is based on service to others will influence your spiritual practice and enhance your spiritual intelligence. "When you appreciate the interconnected nature of all aspects of your life—such as your values, your emotional state—can all contribute to your sense of fulfilment at work, and to your satisfaction and happiness in life" (Dalai Lama). If you believe in the Supreme Being, then you can ask for assistance also, as Guru Gobind Singh does as follows:

> *"O' Lord, of thee this boon I ask;*
> *Let me never shun a righteous task"*

Every choice we make provides us with an opportunity to grow spiritually, to learn what has meaning for us and what is meaningless, what gives us inner peace and what creates inner tensions. Once people begin to live according to their values, their mission in life, their spiritual journey has begun

RICKSHAW WALLAH

You are clearly an expert as far as your life is concerned, regarding your mission and your goals. Your friends and relatives will give you gratuitous advice; they assume that they know it all. Though the advice comes free, we do not have to close our minds. Sometimes we get gems of wisdom from an unexpected source, so it is worth remaining open to new information and possibilities. Let me relate what I learnt from a rickshaw puller in India:

I was young at that time, and I sat in a manual rickshaw because I did not have directions to a certain place. At a steep bank, I got down and pushed the rickshaw when I realized that the going was getting tough for the man. The man was saying something to himself which at first I did not understand. When asked about his soliloquy, the man said that he was addressing his mind which was not under his control. The simple rickshaw wallah explained that he was trying to meditate on God, recite God's name (Naam in Sikhism) but the mind was not concentrating. Some eastern thinkers call the mind a monkey, and he was calling it—*chanchal*—something which is always moving or is restless.

Clearly the simple looking man was meditating or trying to meditate on the supreme power while drawing the rickshaw, while I was sitting at the back and thinking of petty things.

MISSION STATEMENT

'Great leaders like Mahatma Gandhi and Martin Luther often have a clear sense of what it is that they are meant to do, directed to do, and must do.'

There are people like Nelson Mandela, the Dalai Lama, and Archbishop Desmond Tutu who keep the mission in the forefront of their lives whilst performing everyday chores as well. They have made a mark in this world and their views are held in great esteem all over the world for their respective contributions. Some of us lose track of our core values, get lost in the world and feel insecure.

Most of us go through life without a clear sense of purpose or direction. We try a lot of different things, even travel a lot, and have different experiences in life. Yet there is always that restless searching. We seek it, and search different avenues, but never really find exactly what we are supposed to do. The following questions can be of some help in determining your mission or purpose in life. You may wish to reflect deeply on the penetrating questions to realize, and to feel exactly what you are supposed to do. Once you know your motivations, you can write a worthwhile Mission Statement:

1. How would I like to be remembered? The answer could be a calm person who is not easily rattled, man or woman of integrity, a team player, leader, a compassionate person.

2. What do you stand for? (Your principles, ideals, etc.)

3. What message would you be sending to others? You do not have to focus on what others would be thinking of you, but what traits you would be demonstrating in interactions. The answer could be that I am kind, considerate, prepared to listen to others, fair, etc.

4. What am I doing today to make sure that it happens? You can't wait forever for your vision to be realized. Some of us know what we want, but never really do anything about it. The best time to start is today. You may wish to draw up an Action Plan to ensure that you adhere to your Mission State-

ment. If you want to be of service to others, you could start thinking as to how you can render it.

DEATH

Epicurus elucidated death as follows: Death is nothing to us. It is simply the dissolution of the physical elements we are made of, which return to the cosmos they came from. To fear the non-existence that ensues is as irrational as to regret that we did not exist before we were conceived and born. Those who fear death perform an impossible feat, they imagine themselves witnessing their own non-existence, and lamenting it.

Aurelius shares similar views about death and says that human life is a small matter in cosmic terms, and its cycle of life, change and death are inevitable, not to be afraid of and indeed not very important as measured against the scheme of things. If we rationally base our beliefs on what we know to be inevitable, we will suffer neither fear nor anguish.

Death is all around us in nature. Plants grow, and there comes a season when they die. This is the natural law—it's not something new. We humans keep pushing it out of our lives, trying to pretend that we will remain healthy for a long, long time. Like the plants, there are comings and goings, births and deaths. Whether we are ready or not ready, we will die one day. That is what our bodies are meant to do; it is there in the scheme of things. We need to understand our nature and the law of nature. We can contemplate death, and in meditation understand our impermanence on this planet, and to ask, what is it that dies?

If you believe in the immortality of the soul, or after life, then it is only the physical body that expires. If you do not believe in the immortality of the soul, then you can prepare yourself by investigating who you are, the inevitability in the scheme of things. If we are not aware of the inevitability or do not acknowledge it, we live in fear of death. As Socrates said, "Those who love wisdom, practise dying all the time, and death to them is the least terrible thing in the world." Thus exposed to our extinction, we can secure the health of the soul by being compassionate to others and ourselves and it is never too early or too late to secure the health of the soul.

BEING A VICTIM

Quite often we play the role of a victim. I did it because so and so did this to me. I hit him because he was staring at me. This shows that I am a mere actor with no self-determination. We react to outside forces and the 'inside' remains in the dark about the happenings. Only by self-understanding, by being mindful, can we achieve liberation from slavery to outside forces. I am a slave if I am affected by whatever happens externally all the time. Anybody can control my actions and affect my moods and feelings also.

We have the freedom to choose differently and not fit ourselves into what our friends or relatives are doing. Criminology tells us that one of the main factors or motivations which leads most young offenders to get involved in criminal activity is to fit in, to be part of their peer group. After their apprehension by the police, they see themselves as victims rather than perpetrators of an offence. People say, "I just went along with the others," or "I was obeying orders." We make choices all the time. When people shift their orientation from a victim to a creator, their life becomes more interesting. They take responsibility for their behaviour.

We can look at things in different ways, not the way we are programmed or conditioned. We can choose. When we stick to one way of thinking and one way of dealing with issues, we become predictable. We get the programme from our social backgrounds and the family we are born into. It may be a good programme, but why should we be limited or bound by one way of doing things repeating the same old pattern over and over again when we have the opportunity to explore and investigate other options.

Our personal habits are conditioned things, and they are hardly flexible in themselves. If we carry on looking at new experiences through the same perceptions, through the same lens, and never learn to look at things any other way, then we are the victims of our upbringing.

GANDHI

Politics cannot be separated from spiritual values.
Love is the supreme value of life.
All men are brothers because they possess the same soul

—**(Mahatma Gandhi)**

Mahatma Gandhi is an example of a person who did not see himself as a victim but as somebody who was prepared to experiment with a different way of doing things. The basic idea was to bring an end to injustice by changing the heart of the wrongdoer, by awakening through love a sense of justice. One offers love in response to emotional and physical violence. Instead of divide and rule, he chose synergy or combined action: Gandhi included everyone in his efforts to gain independence for India. Traditionally people either continued being victims or resorted to violence. Satyagraha in Sanskrit means—reliance on truth. The path he chose was of passive resistance rather than choosing any one of the traditional ways of fighting injustice. Gandhi experimented with Satyagraha (civil disobedience) both in South Africa and as a leader of the Indian nationalistic movement in India.

His Satyagraha movement raised the consciousness of the Indian masses and made British rule in India more and more untenable, both morally and practically. Gandhi used the word 'ahimsa' which means non-violence, and expanded its meaning so that ahimsa is not just refraining from injuring others, but positively ensuring their well-being, in fact loving them. In a conflict, you can claim to have won only if your opponent can say the same. During one of his visits to London, Gandhi stayed with textile workers who were unemployed because Indians were boycotting manufactured clothes, and the workers cheered him.

The British government attacked and jailed him three times; and he spent seven years in jails for political activity. During one of the high level meetings during the British raj, he suggested to the governor not to allow his (Gandhi's) political activity to "stand between us as men." Thanks to his policy of ahimsa, the transfer of power from the ruler to the ruled was very friendly.

Gandhi never saw himself as a victim, but was an embodiment of non-violence, simplicity, love and caring. In a world full of violence, and swamped by intolerance, his life was a beacon of hope. If only more leaders can say, "All my activities have risen from my insatiable love of mankind"—then the world will be saved.

PLEASURE AND SUFFERING

I am getting what I don't want, and not getting what I want.

As long as we are alive, there will always be people who are going to annoy us, thwart us one way or another. As long as we have desires, or cravings, and they are not met, suffering will be there. If we do not get what we want, unhappiness arises, and even when we get what we want, we always want a little more of it. The cause of discontent could also be: being unable to keep what we have. We want to keep our properties and our wealth with us but are not sure if we can keep them. Most of the time we complain that 'I am getting what I don't want, and not getting what I want.'

When we are unhappy, recognise that it has a cause. And the cause can actually be seen here and now, in our current experience. It doesn't have to be traced back in memory, in time. We think that the cause could have been when someone said those things that were so hurtful. We need to ask, 'what is the present cause in the present moment?' We will always find that it is in our relationship to the currently arising feeling, the way we struggle with it. If we are mindful, conscious of how we are reacting to a certain action, or of our response to a stimulus, we can choose not to react to it the way we are conditioned or habituated to react. We can choose not to allow anyone or anything to take our peace of mind or inner tranquillity.

Guru Nanak in one his famous hymns says: Nanak, the whole world is suffering.

We are living in an era of greed: greed for more wealth, sumptuous food, latest designer clothes, cars and properties. We are never content. People have endless appetites, and are oblivious to the fact that it is wise to be temperate. We have forgotten how to be calm in adverse circumstances or to be philosophical in our lives.

STOICISM

I—smile a hard set smile, like a stoic and let the world have its way. (Tennyson)

Stoicism was a Greek school of philosophy and in the 3rd and 2nd centuries stoics took a prominent part in Greek and Roman revolutionary movements. After the 1st century BC stoicism became the philosophy of the ruling Roman ruling class and lost its revolutionary significance. Such was Stoicism's impact on the Greek and Roman world that it has left its mark on the language we use today—when we describe as stoical or 'philosophical' an attitude of self disciplined, uncomplaining and courageous acceptance of all that life brings. Stoicism has appealed to some of the best and most intelligent minds of the ancient world.

It is a philosophy that enjoins self-mastery and the courage to treat both good and ill fortune as irrelevant to true inner stability of mind.

Self-education in stoic living is to be affected by emulating an ideal wise man—even if such a sage exists only in imagination, and even if one cannot attain that state of moral perfection. The endeavour is the important thing, and the goal is to live in agreement with nature, in the sense of living in conformity with the rational order of things, thereby achieving peace and strength of mind.

The central tenet of Epictetus's teaching was that we must distinguish between what lies within our power and what lies outside our power, learning how to master the former and to accept the latter with fortitude. Only our emotions, thoughts and appetites—our inner mental life are in our power. So we must govern these while cultivating stoic indifference to factors beyond our control. These latter include not only what the world and other people do to us, but some of the ungovernable factors like acts of nature.

The philosophy is quite similar to the Prayer of Serenity, which is:

> *God grant me the serenity to accept the things I cannot change,*
> *Courage to change the things I can,*
> *And wisdom to know the difference. Amen.*

Stoics regarded the passions as natural and said that the way to deal with them properly is to master them by understanding them. Consider the example of fear; reason dictates that we are courageous in the face of danger, but fear does not obey, and makes one run away. Fight or flight are two natural instincts inherited from our ancestors, which helped them in their survival in harsh conditions. Stoicism says that by understanding the true nature of fear, and bringing it under control of self-discipline, one turns it into something positive. It is transformed into carefulness or appropriate caution. In this way the other passions can be converted into what the Stoics call good feelings, among them kindness, generosity and amity.

Plato argued that an ideal city state is one in which each of the community's three orders of citizens—the governors, the guardians or military men and the general population—do what is appropriate for their position in society, and thereby preserve a balance or social harmony between them. Then Plato draws his analogy between the state and the individual. Just as the city has three components, so an individual soul has three parts—reason, the emotions and the appetites. Where these are in harmony, the individual is happy.

YOU HAVE PLENTY!

A wise man was travelling when he observed a young man crying and wailing. The sage stopped and asked the young man the reason for his crying. The young man lamented that he had nothing, no wealth which he could call his own. The wise man said to the young man, "You have plenty, and I will pay you if you give some part of it." The young man was perplexed and asked the sage not to mock at him. The old sage said, "You have two beautiful eyes. I will give you £50,000 if you give me your eyes." The young man thought for a minute, decided that he didn't want to be blind, and declined the offer.

The wise man then said, "If you don't want to give me your eyes, let me have your hands and I will pay you £40,000." When the young man declined to part with his hands, the wise man asked for his feet and offered to pay any price. The young man did not want to be lame so the request was turned down. The wise man then told the young man that he had plenty, but needed to recognise what he had got. Count your blessings instead of thinking of your woes.

SELF DEVELOPMENT—SETTING GOALS

Before setting a goal, be very sure that it is what you **really** want, and it is for yourself. I am saying this so that you do not devote yourself to an aim which may not be after some reflection worthwhile. People do waste themselves in pursuing aims because of the rat race, or what others tell them and once attained find them of no significance. Others are attracted to vacuous pleasures and lose their inner peace because of enslavement to the desire for wealth and fame. Please ask yourself the following questions before embarking on the fulfilment of a goal:

- What does the goal mean to you?

- Why is it important to you?

- Is the goal worthy of you? (Remember that if you are committed to your higher values you would want to lead a worthy life.)

- If it is a material possession you are after, have you considered that it is liable to decay, and that you may have to incur extra costs to maintain or run it?

- What is your real intention in achieving the goal? It could be different from what you think at first. Take some time to consider what your real intention is. For example if it is to write a book, the real intention could be: Be more creative. Or: Make more money. Or: Express yourself.

- If the goal is to run a marathon, the **real** intention might be: Improve your time. Or: Impress others. Or: Avoid spending time with your partner.

A goal is something you wish for, dream about or choose to achieve. It is something you choose to pursue and achieve. Whatever your goals, they must be specific to you, they must be yours and not any body else's.

Charles Muller in *Have anything you Really Really Want!* says that a goal "once implanted visually into your mind—with all of its specific details—takes over and demands realization." Charles Muller should know as he wanted (at the time) a Rolls Royce with walnut picnic tables and achieved exactly what he had visualised!

Being the cautious type, or perhaps a pragmatic person who has had successes and failures in life in equal measure, I hold the view that most goals are achievable, be they personal or to do with material attainments. Most visions can be realized if you have a plan and a streamlined strategy. I wish to emphasise that most goals can be achieved, and most desires can be satisfied, but if some are not realized, please understand that it was not in the scheme of things. Don't fret yourself if failure ensues, but learn lessons from the experience.

Let me mention an instance where I thought setting a goal was essential so that you can decide also when to have a definite Action Plan to work towards milestones and when not to have any deadlines. When young, I was a pretty good swimmer and did my Award of Merit in Life Saving and Silver Medallion in Personal Survival on the same day, just after a rest of about ten minutes. To achieve the Award of Merit, a candidate was expected to rescue two people, retrieve two objects from the bottom of the pool and demonstrate competency in other tasks as well. As regards the Silver medallion, a candidate was expected to swim 40 or 45 lengths of a standard sized pool. It is a long time since I got the Awards, and the requirements may have changed.

Anyway, I went to Mombassa (East Coast of Africa) after a gap of more than 24 years and went straight into the sea for a swim. I had been visualizing myself swimming for long periods as it is easier to swim in the sea than in a swimming pool because of the difference in the density of water. The sea was slightly choppy when I went in, but to my amazement and chagrin, I could not swim even a few yards without stopping for a rest. I thought that it could be because the sea was not calm; it was not conducive to swimming, so I went into a swimming pool and had difficulty in completing two lengths of the small hotel swimming pool.

I had assumed that I still had the strength, fitness and stamina, and proficiency in swimming which I enjoyed in my younger days. How mistaken I was! I had not been in a swimming pool for about two decades and still thought that I could swim without much difficulty. We should not be negative, but our abilities should also be embedded in reality.

Anyway I set a goal for myself which was a short-term goal and in the present tense:

Goal: To swim ten lengths of the pool by the fifth day. (I had only five days to stay at the hotel.)

How:

- To increase two lengths of the small pool every day I swam. (It was measurable.)

- To carry on swimming in the sea as well.

Result:

On the fifth day, I was able to fare much better in the sea at least for an old age pensioner.

So when setting goals, please remember the acronym SMART where S stands for—Specific, M—Measurable, R—Realistic, T—Time limited.

Reality: When I went into the sea and hoped to swim the same way as I used to swim when young, I was not realistic and to use the term in currency at present, it was 'delusional'. I had not entered a swimming pool for more than twenty-four years! I needed to recognise that any sport or game needs continuous practice, other wise one gets rusty. That is the hard reality which I had to acknowledge.

So after coming back from my holiday, I decided to practise swimming on a regular basis. My medium term goal (six months) was to swim 40 lengths of a standard sized swimming pool.

YOU CAN HAVE ANOTHER GO

Any failure seems so total at that time. Later on you realize you can have another go.

At the time of writing this chapter I am observing my granddaughter who is about seven months old. She is learning to walk which is a very difficult skill to master for an infant. She takes a step, takes another step, falls and gets up again. Sometimes she will use the support of a chair or a human hand, but she never gives up. It is fall, get up, fall after two or three steps and get up again. All skills and especially physical skills are learnt and perfected through mistakes and failures.

- Do not be too harsh on yourself when setbacks feature in your life. Ups and downs are natural, part of life. Be compassionate to yourself if others are unrestrained in their criticism.

- Try to understand that what is lost by not trying and what is lost by not succeeding are two different things.

- Failure is rarely **real** failure. Real failure occurs only when one is unwilling to understand its role.

- It is impossible for us to be always successful, capable and accomplished in different areas of our life.

- Errors in whatever we do are inevitable. We need to accept that every setback and every error has a role as a teacher.

HOW

Some of the questions you can ask yourself when going over a past failure are:

- What can I learn here? (Identify what you have learnt from your failure.)

- What can I do differently next time?

- How can I use the adversity in a positive way to bounce back?

- What are my options?

- Which option is most likely to lead to success?

DEALING WITH FAILURE

After a failure, hope may be in short supply for a while if you ruminate with those who have succumbed to similar failures; they will only reinforce the view that nothing can be done about it. Following are some helpful hints to deal with failure:

- **Pervasiveness/catastrophes**—is expecting the worst and interpreting events as evidence of impending disaster. Some people see a setback as a total disaster, which will affect their total life. If such thoughts occur, recognise that they are automatic negative thoughts, i.e. they occur very swiftly, and without apparent prior cogitation or pondering. There is no Stop and Think, Automatic Negative Thoughts are prevailing. To fail means to give up. Anything else is simply a temporary setback and usually a great learning experience

- **Define the problem**: Instead of focusing on how terrible the problem is, concentrate on defining the problem as a basis of solving the problem. (See Problem Solving.)

- **Wishful Thinking**: When the outcome is not to our satisfaction, we tend to indulge in wishful thinking. There is a "classic destination syndrome" which assumes that when you reach the heaven of success, all your troubles will disappear. It is unlikely that you will get everything right every time. Treat the failure as a challenge rather than dwelling on how wonderful life would have been if the failure hadn't occurred.

- **Challenges**: Success will not end your troubles. As soon as one problem is solved, another will appear, or as soon as one goal is reached, another will be set sooner or later, and challenges start all over again. As Winston Churchill said: "Happiness is not freedom from problems, but happiness is having problems and handling them, and learning how to grow in order to handle them."

- **Be resilient**: Resilient people rise again after experiencing blue times. If you find it difficult to bounce back, observe others who have faced similar failures and survived them. Discuss with them how they managed to overcome their failures with a view to learning something from them.

- **Measured Response**: There is a certain virtue to not appearing to take things too seriously. You can laugh about it with others. Treat the whole thing with unflinching gravity, and it will be difficult to explain to others why you failed.

- **Higher Power**: If you believe that you have done everything that was possible, believe that the Higher Power or Nature has other plans for you or a Master Plan.

- **Analyse**: To move forward, look at the problem or yourself realistically and **identify aspects of yourself that you know you must change**. To turn failure into success, look for support around you. An effective Life Coach can be a catalyst to solutions, and help you when you perceive that the path to moving forward in life is blocked.

RIGHT FOCUS

After setting the goal, I found myself thinking all the time whether I would be able to achieve my goal. I had all the negative self-talk swamping me, and it was accompanied by physical fear and tiredness. I had to overcome the internal blocks, like fatigue in the initial stages, fear of not achieving the goal, and keeping up my motivation level, etc.

I was not concentrating on the strokes, but on the number of lengths I had to do. I had to remind myself that I had not swum for a long time and I had to master the technique. Total focus and concentration was needed on perfecting my stroke to achieve the best performance. So instead of thinking of completing 40 lengths, I concentrated on the Breaststroke, which is my favourite stroke, moment **by moment.** When swimming, I still focus on generating force during the propulsive phase by:

1. The arm stroke

2. The kick

3. Timing of the arm stroke and kick

4. Body position

5. Breathing.

So whatever your goal, it may be to do with performance in sports or self development, focus on the event or task, moment by moment. Be present in every moment and you will have the toughness and psychological skills to work for you rather than against you.

WHEN SETTING DEADLINES IS NOT NECESSARY

A colleague of mine asked if I had set any deadlines—had any short term or medium term goals regarding the completion of this book. I told him that writing the book ultimately was my dream, and my responsibility. I was committed to quality and perfection as far as possible. My strategy in this case was to gather all the necessary knowledge and facts, by reading and research. It was a long journey and I was learning a lot about myself. I wanted to share my experiences with others. My aim or long-term goal was to help people have a better life, tranquillity in life, and I wanted to suggest methods that WORK and are effective. In this case I had a strategy, a plan but no deadlines.

I still break down other Goals into smaller achievable goals and set deadlines, etc., like I did to improve my swimming. As regards the writing of this book, I did visualize it in its completed form. When you visualize, your mind is focused on what you want; it is probably a major step towards making it concrete. When you visualize your goal, it becomes embedded in your subconscious. Though it is a long-term goal, the idea is firmly planted and embedded.

SEE PROBLEMS AS TEACHERS

> *When you see the problems as teachers, you learn the lesson, become mature and grow strong.*
>
> —**(Wisdom for a Peaceful Life)**

We only win when we are able to handle loss, to tolerate and accept failure. Great people have cultivated over a period of years a high tolerance for mistakes, setbacks and failures. They tolerate failure, and then become better by being able to see their way out of the storm.

When we accept failure, we relax, learn and forge ahead. Jerry Lynch in *Creative Coaching* offers this advice: "To learn to gain, we must actively embrace failure, and use it as a tool for eventual success." You will never feel too disappointed or suffer much agony if you use your failures as building blocks for future success. Most often we fail to turn defeat into eventual victory and crises into an opportunity to improve because we do not have a clear perspective. We do not see things clearly because we are overwhelmed by our failure, we do not see setbacks as our best teacher.

Some psychologists say that 'learning lessons' has become a cliché. When any mishap happens, or things do not go according to plan, those responsible say that they have learnt lessons. With critical analysis, and self-awareness, which encourages us to take responsibility for our mistakes, a failure learned from can be transformed into a success. With the right attitude, there need not be any real failures, only learning experiences put to good use in life. Sometimes it is difficult to be objective when we have a vested interest. We all have our blind spots; there are areas where we lack proper understanding and cannot be impartial. We come up with the same explanations and views. We become rigid in our thinking.

In such cases it is better to consult significant others—people you trust or professionals. This habit has to be cultivated, as we all like to depend on our judgement and conclusions. With formal or informal feedback, we can get a better description of the things as they are and not the way we imagine them to be. A reasoned feedback based on logic and analysis can help us to grow and develop.

We can learn from our experiences in retrospect, by examining the results of our actions, whether ultimately they resulted in reaching our goal or not, and whether they caused any harm to oneself or others. The retrospective approach may not change the outcomes of our mistakes, but it can certainly lead us to a better self-understanding and shape our attitudes and behaviour in a more positive direction.

Be creative in thinking how you can benefit from your failures, or grasp the principle. **Forget the troubles of the past and move forward with the lessons learned.**

WHY PROBLEMS ARISE

When something happens in the world that is in sync with our desires, we love it or like it. When external happenings are not in consonance with our desires, with what we feel should be happening or not happening, we do not like it, and feel disturbed. We are pushed by the desires from the past, things which we have not been able to acquire so far and worry about the future because we are not sure if we will get them. A poet has described the past as a rock face and the future as a rock. The mind is everywhere, but never in the present. We forget that the night that has passed, is gone; it is our past, and tomorrow is another day.

The fluctuations result in a roller coaster ride, up and down, and there is no mental or emotional equanimity. In other words, when the body and mind go through the fluctuations, we feel sad or depressed.

One solution is to rise above all that affects you so easily to a higher realm. The problems arise because of our bondage, our attachment to physical and emotional comfort from external sources. If we retain our inner independence, then the others do not have the power to influence change in us, to make us sad, angry or depressed. It can only happen if we learn to withdraw into the oasis of peace and tranquillity within us.

With self-awareness, we can learn to recognise these changes that the mind and body are experiencing.

LEARNING FROM AN EXPERIENCE

You learn from your painful experiences when you decide to change your way of doing things because you do not want to create the same experiences again.

To learn from an experience, remember an occasion when you were very upset, angry, shocked, or felt at a complete loss. While you are reliving this experience, remember how you acted. Focus your attention on your behaviour and feelings only. Some question and tips which will help you to learn are:

- Did you cry, rage, withdraw, feel confused or become sad?

- What sensations are you feeling in your body? (Feel the sensations in your body while revisiting the experience.)

- What did you do? A…. B…. C …

- Say to yourself, "I intend to learn everything from this experience. **I take responsibility for my mistakes."**

- What could you have done differently?

- Now imagine yourself acting differently with harmony in mind, or cooperation in mind or respect for the other person in mind.

The patterns in your life require your choices. They will not change merely because you desire or wish them to change. They require action, your willingness to make responsible choices and put them into practice. You harvest what you plant. Responsible choice is choosing the harvest before you plant. A gardener can't plant nettles and then expect sweet grapes.

NEW CHOICES—NEW EXPERIENCES

Your experiences become similar and predictable when you choose without thinking—you will act like you have done in the past. You can always choose to break the pattern; you do not have to follow the same mode of practice or procedure. When you make the connection between your choices and your experiences, you do not have to create the same experiences again. You can create different experiences by choosing differently. You are not limited, you have the potential to change, the intellect to think differently. If you have reacted angrily when somebody said something unpleasant, you can respond differently the next time by not speaking in anger or fear. You can choose a different mode of behaviour.

When we see our life as meaningless, view ourselves as powerless, look at people we interact with as vile or bad, we create painful experiences. When we see our life as meaningful, perceive ourselves as loving, compassionate, a creative spirit, and look at the world as kind and helpful, we create a healthy and pleasant experience. What experience you want to create is your choice.

When choosing a behaviour you want to change, or would like to experiment with to have different experiences, try the following:

- Recall what consequences the behaviour or reaction has created in the past.

- Decide if now is the time to change this behaviour or reaction.

- Make a choice that will create consequences that are more appropriate.

- If you find yourself repeating the same behaviour, or reacting in a similar manner, be gentle with yourself and start the process again. Decide how you will choose next time.

- Imagine yourself making the healthier choices.

- Make choices based on your high values. For example, you can choose futures of harmony, cooperation, sharing, etc.

- **Your optimal choice is the choice your soul makes.**

CALM COOL AND CONFIDENT

Most of us want to be calm, cool and confident in most situations. When you are calm, confident and cool, you are at peace with yourself, you accept yourself. Please reflect on the following questions to find out how you express yourself in the following situations:

1. How do you cope with failure?

2. How do you handle pressure in your workplace and at home?

3. How do you exhibit patience and mindfulness in your everyday life?

4. When and how do you give respect to others?

5. How do you cope with criticism?

6. Do you often try to serve others? What do you do?

7. Do you accept responsibility for your behaviour?

8. How do you ensure that the decisions you make are sound ones?

CONFIDENCE

Most of us inevitably experience failures, setbacks and loss. It is part of life and needs to be accepted as such. However with repeated setbacks, discouragement can set in, causing us to lose confidence. When feeling distraught, focusing your attention on your inadequacies can only complicate an already confidence depleting situation. You can prevent this happening by finding creative ways to focus on your strengths and the possibilities you have.

Some people say that they are always confident, but some mental obstacles are natural. Before undertaking any major job, self-doubt, fear, anxiety, do raise their heads. Mindfulness can help you to clear your mind, and ignore external distractions up to a large extent. It frees us from mental and emotional obstacles. With this mental practice, you are not thinking of the outcomes, it allows you to focus on the present. When you concentrate on the present only, you are more relaxed, more productive, and more focused on the task in hand.

Another strategy is to focus on your inner world. It is a journey to discover your own battles against fear, failure, and self-doubt. If you succeed, it is a battle over inner conflict, it is mastery over yourself. When we think of things we can't control, we become anxious, tension builds up and confidence decreases. How can you have confidence in something you can't control? When you shift to things you can control—your desire, commitment, confidence, preparedness, boldness, enthusiasm, etc., then you are in-charge, and the **confident YOU** can perform at a better level.

The challenge is within, the real opponent is not out there, it is one's self. If you are not striving for the impossible, examine your limiting beliefs, and acknowledge that they are beliefs and not facts. Ask yourself 'How valid is my limiting belief?' and change the belief to its opposite and see how effective it becomes. Once you are aware of your limiting thoughts and beliefs, you can change them into positive ones, 'I can'—instead of 'I can't'. You are probably doing what you want to do, so have fun and enjoy the moment.

When you develop your ability to achieve your goals and work through adversity, setback or failures, your confidence increases. It is a victory over your inner battles, and the reward is deeply private and personal.

HOW

- Don't think too much as to whether it is possible, but rather **how** it is possible

- Believe in your power, the inner strength to demonstrate your ability and do your best.

- Direct your attention away from the outcome and toward developing a sense of the inner self.

- Think of your tangible and intangible strengths. Write them down. Refer to your strengths when you feel despondent to uplift your spirits.

- Focus on the present. Live in the precious moment. Enjoy the process. You can think of the outcome at the right moment.

- See setbacks and failures as learning opportunities. If you persist through many setbacks and obstacles to achieve your dream, to be what you want to be, you will be enriched by the experience of trying. You may not achieve world success, but it will be internal success.

- People with low commitment or lack of confidence, often see their setbacks as justification to abandon their dreams. Give yourself permission to make mistakes, knowing that you can learn from them.

- If you have a dream, you need to act to realize it. Remember that alongside your 'I can' attitude, hard work is also essential.

- **Nothing builds confidence like success**. Set short-term realistic attainable goals. Each task/job when performed successfully results in big things happening.

- Reward yourself. Recognise your achievements, your excellence and try to build on it.

- Repeat the affirmation: 'I am calm and confident.'

IMAGERY

Past successes are wonderful confidence builders and reinforcers. Recall successful execution of jobs, notice how you did the task, assignment, did the presentation, or met the deadline with total confidence. Use these experiences as material to visualize how well you can deliver what you were expected to do. Remind yourself that if you were capable of doing so well in the past, you can repeat or improve upon that level of performance.

AFFIRMATIONS

To affirm is to assert strongly, to state as a fact. Affirmations are statements or expressions that describe the way you want to be. They are expressions that give you permission to change self-defeating patterns of thought into positive reinforcements.

Use the following guidelines to create your own affirmations:

1. The statements should be positive stating precisely what you want rather than what you don't want. Negative statements create anxiety and self-doubt which hinder your progress.

2. The sentence should be short, precise and personal.

3. The expression should be in the present tense; rather than saying "I will be calm", say :

    - "I am calm."

    - "I appreciate myself."

    - "I am confident."

4. Act as if the affirmation were true.

5. Use words that have emotions and actions, words that are meaningful to you.

Write the expressions on a card or cards and place them in a draw which you use quite often. Read the affirmations twice or thrice a day. Visualize or picture what they say. Imagine what you would feel when you are calm and confidant. Imagine what you would hear. Imagine what you would see when you are not perturbed by external forces.

When you choose differently, you create differently.

SUPPORTING YOUNG PEOPLE

In this decade, lack of discipline and unruly behaviour by young people is very much in the news. Publications of official figures showing the number of children expelled from schools, especially from larger ones, have soared. Teachers are at a loss as to how to maintain discipline in the classes and it is driving them away from their profession. I have worked as a teacher in a primary, and a secondary school, and as a tutor in a Teachers' College. I have also had a stint in the probation service first as a main grade officer and then as a Treatment Manager of a One-to-One programme where I had to deal with young people who were disaffected with education and had gone off the rails.

We all need acceptance, irrespective of our age, a sense of belonging, to a family, a team or a school. When dealing with others, and especially young people, compliments and positive comments about their efforts are important for their development. It will be a big booster in their quest to be the best, be it in sports or studies. Giving young persons timely praise and attention supports their efforts to perform or work at their optimal level. With negative comments, the young person will feel inadequate, unworthy and it will lower their confidence. When remarking on a young persons' work, or providing feedback, focus on the positive steps they have taken towards improvement. Reinforce and nurture the good behaviour and their strengths which have come to light.

Instead of focusing on what they have failed to do, comment on what has been done or achieved. Those who are complimented and praised, tend to put in more effort to achieve personal success. Look for ways to demonstrate your confidence in the person's abilities.

If you consider that the young person lacks awareness of the mistakes being committed, you may want to point out what they need to focus on. Try to show to the person that your confidence is still intact even if he has made a mistake.

You can become a more effective father, mother, guardian, coach or leader by searching for ways to satisfy the emotional and psychological needs of those you are trying to nurture or train.

USEFUL HINTS

- It has long been established that rewards are more effective than punishment in motivating young people

- With affirmations and rewarding of positive behaviour, they are likely to have a strong foundation of self-esteem.

- If you want to discipline a young person, avoid reprimanding in front of others.

- Talk to them as to how a mistake can be corrected or prevented from happening again in the future instead of labouring on why it was committed.

The following abbreviated 'Inspiration' pointers sum up very elegantly how children learn what they live:

If a child lives with criticism,
He learns to condemn.
If a child lives with hostility,
He learns to fight.
If a child lives with ridicule,

He learns to be shy
If a child lives with tolerance,
He learns to be patient.
If a child lives with encouragement,
He learns confidence.
If a child lives with praise,
He learns to appreciate.
If a child lives with approval,
He learns to like himself.
If a child lives with acceptance and friendship,
He likes to find love in the world.

PERSONAL SATISFACTION

We worry too much about being successful and pleasing others—husband, wife, partner, parents, line manager, supervisor, etc. We build up layers of anxiety and stress because we do not have much control over the outcome. When you complete a task, or an assignment, whether the output is appreciated by your line manager or supervisor, is not within your control. Focus on the things that you can control instead, your expertise or skills, attitude to that particular piece of work and mind set.

If you have done your best, that could be a victory for you. 'A well done' by a boss may sometimes sound shallow and is transitory. Your personal satisfaction of having given your best shot is more important. If you have a commitment to high standards, and have worked hard, been diligent, then you know that you are focussed on your strengths and not others' approval.

OBSERVE—REFLECT—LEARN

Don't look back in anger and fret over it, explore what lessons you can draw from the experience instead.

Usually we dismiss unhappy experiences as unwanted experiences. We suppress them or ignore them but rarely learn from them. An unwanted experience can be an opportunity to learn. We do not learn from pleasant experiences as well, we just get lost in them, enjoy them. It is only the painful observations or experiences that goad us to wake up.

We can learn from pleasant and the unpleasant experiences, or the wanted and the unwanted experiences.

What can you learn when you see an old frail man walking or a sick man on a bed? Gautma Buddha was born in a royal household. On separate occasions he saw a sick man, an old man, and a dead man. These were disturbing experiences for Gautma. He thought these conditions awaited him and wondered how to escape them. On his fourth trip outside the palace, he saw a sadhu or an ascetic who was seeking the Truth. Gautma abandoned his wife, son and the royal household and embarked on extreme asceticism.

Baba Buddha (not to be confused with Gautma Buddha) is famous in Sikhism because at the age of seven or eight years only he observed that small tender branches burn faster than the thick sturdy and old ones when thrown onto a bonfire. He related his observation to his own life and thought that death could visit him whilst he was very young. The young man became a follower of Guru Nanak. (Baba is a term of endearment for an old man in Punjabi. Guru Nanak gave the honorific to Baba Buddha for his observations and wisdom.)

You do not have to be an academic to acquire 'true knowledge'. In some cases an illiterate person may have it. Some of the greatest saints and wise people have come from humble backgrounds, but have had unique insight. It is said that Buddha got Enlightenment whilst sitting under a pipal tree. It has to do with inner perception, recognising the difference between the 'real and the unreal.'

> *"The wise man, I affirm, can find no rest in that which perishes, Nor will lend his heart to 'ought' which doth on time depend ..."*
>
> —(Wardrobe)

People acquire knowledge and parrot it. If it is 'true knowledge', it should be reflected upon so that we understand its real significance and **live it.**

> *Let knowledge grow from more to more*
> *But more of reverence in us dwell ...*

CHANGE

Change' is scientific, 'progress' is ethical; change is indubitable, whereas progress is a matter of controversy

　　—(Unpopular Essays (1950): 'Philosophy and Politics')

Everyone thinks of changing the world, but nobody thinks of changing himself or herself.

People do change, some for the better and unfortunately some for the worse. As regards changing for the better, it often happens as people weigh up the pros and cons of carrying on as they are and come to a rational conclusion that change is needed. It is a logical, wilful decision, reached after some real soul searching. If we don't change, we don't grow. If we don't grow, then we are not living our life to its full potential.

Change for Confucius was something inevitable and necessary, and taken as a basic fact. However it is not easy to change, even though we accept that the world is changing all the time. We do not want to step out of our 'comfort zone'. We are used to our patterns of behaviour and possibly not even aware of them. They are our habits, and habits are difficult to change

Change can take time, though sometimes it hits you unannounced and comes like a bolt after bereavement or some extraordinary experience. Anyway, generally speaking, you are in charge of the change you want to bring about. The desirable form of change is normally gradual reform rather than sudden or a violent disruption coming out of the blue. Some people with a tendency to think rigidly or who are impatient by nature claim that change does not happen. Patience is essential for anyone who wants to change something in his or her life. It could be self-knowledge, a more fulfilling career, better education, responsible citizenship, interpersonal relationships, etc.

When there is outside pressure for us to change, our normal feelings are—anger and denial. It is difficult to accept that we need to change. Only with self-analysis, there may be some guarded acceptance that change is needed. One has to take responsibility for one's learning and personal development, but there is always a reluctance to do it.

With contemplation, dissatisfaction can occur, because an individual besides other things looks at the negative and the positive parts, the way things are—and the way things could be. Discrepancy can also arise between the current state of affairs and the value system embraced by the individual. Even when one has contemplated change, it is difficult to take a firm decision to change. We are all good at rationalizing and not doing anything about our intentions. It is like climbing a mountain.

When people reach the decision stage, to uncover the best in them, they are prepared to temper and experiment or try new patterns of behaviour. Sometimes it is a simple decision also, a decision based on simple logic or commonsense. People weigh up the pros and cons of carrying on as they are and come to the rational conclusion that change is needed. This sets the process of change in motion.

Acceptance and willingness to remould and redirect some strong parts of the personality follows after a person has gone through a 'willing trial.' But the desirable form of reform needs to be gradual rather than a violent disruption otherwise it will be difficult to maintain it. For example, if you want to get fit, it would be better to start with short walks rather than going for long distance running.

In order for anything to happen in life there must be motivation, not inertia, and the realization that you want to be somebody different—to have a meaningful life—can be a big motivator. Motivation is the prime mover of every human activity. Emotions drive motivation. After all they share the same Latin root, "to move". Emotions mobilise action. They also give it direction and force. Only with motivation can you maintain the change. To change, one needs 'learnt optimism', a positive disposition or 'can do' attitude.

When change occurs, it is not that the body changes or one becomes taller or shorter. Life will be the same, but it is how one looks at things that changes. Change sweeps through the individual's behaviour, attitudes and thought processes. If it is a paradigm change, the transformation could be at the level of personality, of core guiding principles, at the way of understanding reality and life on this planet.

Anyone who has worked with 'reformed' offenders or recovered alcoholics knows the reality that people do change. It is also a reality that some people do not change. It must be acknowledged that there are offenders also who do not change and alcoholics who do not give up the misuse of alcohol. Some people remain angry, vengeful, narrow minded and bigoted throughout their lives. They react repeatedly in the same way because of their psychological and emotional characteristics and create the same experiences and same consequences. Others replace the anger with calmness or lighten up, vengeance with appreciation of the humanity of the 'perceived enemy,' narrow mindedness with understanding and knowledge. If one wants to change, it has to be a wilful decision.

SOME USEFUL HINTS

1. Change should not be for its own sake; one should have a vision in mind.

2. Nobody can change you. Real change is a voluntary activity. Only you can take the decision to change.

3. When making a change, one must have a clear vision or a goal. Without a clear goal you might experience feeling muddled.

4. Quite often we focus on the wrong things. Your vision is not a haphazard affair; it needs to be underpinned by values, principles and clear achievable targets.

5. Change will only survive if we live it and are inspired by it.

WAYS TO BRING ABOUT CHANGE

• De-programme your mind from everything you have been doing to allow it be open. Open it up to be able to be taught, to look at things dispassionately.

• Ask yourself:

   1. Why do you want to make a change?

   2. What will change?

   3. What will it look like when the change has happened?

   4. What will it feel like when the goal has been achieved?

• If you want to change, be prepared to step out of your comfort zone, and take risks.

- Keep in mind that to sustain change, you must truly love what you are doing. There is enthusiasm for whatever you are doing. Your heart and soul must be in it. If not, you may not experience real success.

- When you feel your enthusiasm fade, remind yourself why you decided to transform your life.

- Just don't give up trying to do what you really want to do. Where there is love and inspiration, I don't think you can go wrong. (Ella Fitzgerald.)

- Be creative to sustain the change.

5

Stress

Stress is a physical or mental demand that provokes certain responses in us, allowing us to meet challenges or escape danger. A moderate amount of stress can improve your performance in situations such as sports and work, but excessive stress can harm your health. People who feel very stressed may be anxious, tearful, irritable or low in spirits. Sleep may be disrupted and relationships may suffer.

As regards the heart, stressful situations trigger immediate increase in levels of the hormone adrenaline and boost heart rate. These subside gradually when conditions return to normal. Scientists say that the body defends the heart from damage caused by stress through a system called the autonomic nervous system. However, repeatedly high levels of stress causes wear and tear, undermining this so called heart rate variability—the heart's natural defence mechanism.

Traumatic or stressful events happen in our lives, all the time; some do not affect us much but then others are more serious and impacting. Death, losing a loved one, redundancy, divorce, changing jobs, moving house—they all affect us in different ways, and our ability to cope varies from person to person. It depends upon the type of person we are, how strongly we feel at the time when the situation arises or the level of stress we are experiencing.
Clare Evans, a writer on stress, says that there are six main stages when somebody is dealing with a stressful event:

1. Shock and Denial: When we hear bad news, we experience shock, denial, confusion, fear, numbness and blame, etc.

2. Anger/Resistance: This often follows after the initial shock.

3. Dialogue/Bargaining: As we start to come to terms with the situation, we are more likely to be able to talk about it.

4. Depression: Some people have reported sleeplessness, early morning waking and other symptoms of depression. The person experiencing emotional upheaval may feel overwhelmed and have a sense of helplessness.

5. Acceptance: This is the stage when the person is ready to move on and is able to accept what has happened.

6. Return to normality: In some cases 'normality' may not be possible, but once the situation has been accepted, moving forward to a more secure and strong position is once again possible.

If you are experiencing a stressful time, the above chart may help you to recognise where you are and that it is not wrong to feel these emotions.

COPING WITH STRESS

> *It is our evaluation of events, not the events themselves that determine our emotional and behavioural reactions to these events.*
>
> —(Neenan and Palmer)

People lead stressful lives and have a vision of a golden or peaceful time, somewhere in the future when they can put stress behind them and life will make sense. They dream of moving to a different place, change the job or retire. We search for a stress-free life, but with most of us the dream never comes true.

Andy Secombe, author of *Endgame* who with his family searched for a stress-free life from the depths of despair, says that: "My condition taught me that true happiness and contentment are not dependent on externals. The search for the simple life is an inward journey. We may never find that dream cottage (place), but we are finding something much more important—ourselves."

Some suggestions to cope with stress:

• We get stressed when we do not get the outcome or reward we expected. Most of us get attached to the fruit of our actions. (See 'Attachment' in Chapter 1). Put in your full effort in whatever you are doing but do not be attached to the outcome. If you do not get the result you expected, remember that it is not total failure. You can always have another go.

- Make a list of what you gained from your experience. Every experience is a learning opportunity. All the positives will help you to move forward towards tranquillity.

- Make a list of all the mistakes you believe you have made and all your regrets. Acknowledge your feelings. After writing down the list, be willing to forgive yourself and let go of your negative thoughts and feelings.

- Acknowledge that the experience like everything else in life is impermanent, and forgiveness of yourself and learning from the experience is part of the letting go process. Thus you can learn to switch off at the end of the day.

- After a stressful event write a diary for one or two months. Write the journal every day if possible till you feel that you have gained your old serenity and calmness. Describe your feelings, moods and insights. This will enable you to get your feelings out of your system and onto paper and put them in perspective.

- Try the 0 to 100 trick—ask yourself how important the problem is in the context of your life. If the score is less than 50, it may not be worth getting stressed over it after all.

- Learn 'selective blindness' so that you are able to ignore or turn a blind eye to certain sources of stress.

- If the stress level persists, take stress reduction as seriously as your work. Talk with people you are comfortable with, your friends or relatives about your stress level and your feelings.

- If you consider that your friend or significant other will not be able to understand you, get some professional coaching or counselling. Talking with a professional can help you get the bottled up feelings out. The professional should be objective, someone who can work to help you to manage or reduce the stress level.

If you deny or run away from the stress feelings, they stay with you forever. The quicker you can learn to deal with your feelings, the quicker you will be able to move forward to a more meaningful existence. It's only by experiencing them that you can let them go. It is only by letting go that you can be truly free.

ARE YOU UNDERCHALLENGED?

We all talk of being overstressed because of work or too many demands being made on us. Another form of stress is being under-challenged. Busy people often forget to build in time for themselves, to grow and develop mentally. Exercising your brain is just as important as going to the gym or pursuing any sport or regime. If we do not work our minds, it can result in a psychological state where we feel bored, and we start to feel wound up. It is because we are not learning anything new or being adventurous in life.

Scientific research shows that if you don't use your brain, it will start to shut down, and your memory and creativity will be affected. People even reach a point where they lose enthusiasm for life. Who wants to talk to a bored person who has nothing new to say? People avoid uninteresting persons. However, if you are full of ideas, and energy, people will gravitate towards you. Maintaining an active mind keeps you both interesting and interested.

If you feel that you are stressed because you are under-challenged, carry out a personal audit:

• Make a list of all your current skills, strengths and passions.

• Make a list of what's missing in your life, or would like to have more often, something which really motivates you, which will bring some fulfilment to your life. Thinking about 'what you are now' and 'what you could be' or 'what is' and what ought to be," will manifest the skill or knowledge you consider you want to acquire or needs strengthening. It could be to do with art, creative writing, literature, etc.

SOME USEFUL SUGGESTIONS

• Notice if there is any inner talk, is it negative, positive or perhaps both? Ditch the negative thinking. Set your mind free—you are never too old, too young or not talented enough to learn a new skill. These are self-imposed limitations. If you are worried about failing, change your thinking. Say to yourself, "This is for me."

• Let go of your fear just a little, and become willing to take the next step.

• Have a belief in yourself. Trust yourself and look forward to the new challenge.

- Focus on getting your brain working and on realizing your potential.

- Set realistic targets.

- If you are in a relationship, talk with your partner. You will have a positive connection if you are buddies in self-improvement.

- If you can't be companions, or can't have a shared target, let people around you know about your commitment. Sometimes friends and family can be your worst enemies when you try to make a few changes and they are suspicious of them or don't like them

STRESSFUL LIFE EVENTS

CHRISTMAS PRESSURE

Christmas, according to *A Christmas Carol* (1843) by Charles Dickens, is a good time: a kind forgiving, charitable, pleasant time: the only time I know in the long calendar of the year when men and women seem by one consent to open their shut-up hearts freely, and to think of people below them as if they really were fellow passengers to the grave.

Today's Christmas with its insistent commercial pressure, its accretion of modern adornments—from electronic toys to almost violent Boxing Day sales—seems a long way from Dickens's sentiments.

It is estimated that on average mothers spends 13 days preparing for Christmas. It is a fact most of the stocking fillers are from China. In the month of November 2006, 45000 tonnes of items 'made in China' were delivered to Britain's shelves.

The prevalent feeling is that we ought to be happy at Christmas. Nothing short of unbridled jollity will do. There is pressure to be perfectly happy, preferably surrounded by smiling ones. In real life it can be a minefield. I must say that I am writing this essay as somebody looking in from the outside, so I can be quite objective. I am comfortable in Eastern and Western cultures as I have relations and friends in both of them.

People shop day and night till they are physically and emotionally exhausted. People really get stressed as they desperately seek the presents on their list or 'must have ones'. An investigation by a national newspaper in England found that the heartbeat of a married couple soared from the resting state of 70 beats a minute (bpm) to over 100 per minute in the days leading up to Christmas!

Somebody wrote that they become fatter and poorer during the festive season. Fatter because they eat too much, and poorer because of the number of presents they have to buy. Some families pay their Christmas debts for the whole of the following year and the vicious cycle starts again. Crime increases during Christmas time because of the pressure on offenders to be part of the festivities. Its observance is first attested in Rome in the year 336. Christmas absorbed the festive atmosphere of the Roman Saturnalia and the other pagan festivals it replaced, and since then it has continued to accumulate 'traditions', particularly in the 19th century.

We tend to forget what Christmas is all about in our anxiety to get it right. A survey carried out by 'Theos UK', the religious think tank, found that for 62 per cent Christmas made them think of spiritual matters. And for 77 per cent, it made them think about what is "important". Communication Research polled 1000 adults and 86 per cent rated spending time with family and friends as the best thing about Christmas.

Please ask yourself:

1. What does Christmas mean to you?

2. What does Christmas mean to your family? (Ask them.)

3. How can you accommodate their needs?

IS CHRISTMAS TOO COMMERCIAISED?

There is so much perceived pressure from everyone—family and friends—to create a perfect Christmas. Accommodating everyone's needs is a challenging task in the lead up to Christmas. Again in the study by Theos, 89 per cent of people believed that Christmas was too commercialised. Most people find the financial pressure as the worst thing about Christmas.

HELPFUL SUGGESTIONS TO CUT THE PRESSURE

- If you want to buy presents for family and friends, start shopping early and spread your spending. Set a realistic budget and stick to it.

- Try not to become a prisoner of the inescapable tradition of the perfect Christmas. You are probably following a tradition which started in the 19th century. Make your own 'tradition'.

- Think of others but do not force your idea of Christmas on them.

- The stress of Christmas comes from the idea of how it should be. Try to be flexible. You do not have to follow the same routine every year. Families can discuss different arrangements and try them out. A new format could be: Instead of the Big Lunch, you can spend the money on pantomime tickets. It would give you an opportunity to get out of the house.

- Instead of sitting at home, you can go for a brisk walk to admire the trees and lights or simply be with nature.

- Find time for **yourself** to relax, time to unwind, if you do not want to be worn out by cooking and trying to keep everyone happy.

- Christmas is supposed to be a time of goodwill. If you have relatives or friends staying with you, remember that they are there only for a day or two.

- Above all RELAX. Don't make such a big deal out of Christmas that people tense up and can't enjoy it.

- People should not feel under pressure to come for Christmas. There is no fun in spending half of your holiday on the motorway. If your close ones cannot be with you, you can always converse with them on the telephone.

- It is not a disaster if the old folk have to spend Christmas on their own. They may be perfectly happy.

ACCIDENTS

According to the Royal Society for the Prevention of Accidents (U.K) approximately 80,000 people end up in casualty over the 12 days of Christmas. Accidents happen, and people fall down from steps or stairs when inebriated.

- Some people think that Christmas holidays are for drinking only or a national licence to get drunk every day during the festive season. There is no point in having a hangover and ending up in a hospital. It is hardly 'fun' to sweat at A&E for three hours before you are seen to.

- One drink becomes a bottle. If drinking is one of your tightropes, one drink can lead to many more.

- If you do not have a dependency on alcohol or illicit drugs, you can regulate yourself so that it remains social drinking and not self-indulgence.

- Think of your family. It is a time of goodwill. Your family does not have to worry unduly while you are hitting the bottle.

WEDDINGS: WHY HAVE THEY BECOME SO GROTESQUE?

Marriage is generally taken to be the union of two people in which commitment is made and responsibility undertaken. Marriage is not a mere private liaison. It is a public, legally recognised declaration of a union that is joining two families. It is a statement to say, 'thy people shall be my people.' It is an undertaking by the couple to their parents as well as their offspring, as well as to the wider community; as well that they are willing to advance themselves economically, spiritually and are willing to take their share of the communal load.

It is gaining prominence again as practically all the studies show that marriage is more enduring than cohabitation. The statistical support for this proposition is now so crushing as to extinguish any rational argument to the contrary. This is not a moralistic condemnation of existing single parents or people living together, or an attempt to impose a pattern of personal life on the population. It is simply a statement of hard fact based on empirical evidence. The value of marriage is unquestionable and the ceremony should be an enjoyable occasion rather than a stressful event. What follows is mainly for couples that have decided to take the big step. People get married mainly because:

- Marriage is an integral part of their culture or religious beliefs and an essential part of their core value system.

- It is a celebration of love between two people and a declaration of devotion to each other.

- Consider that marriage is the right environment in which to start a family.

- They want their family and friends to share in their happiness and commitment as a couple.

• The couple have discussed the issue over a long period and they want to go ahead with a firm bond in place.

EMOTIONAL AND FINANCIAL IMPLICATIONS

The crunch comes when you want a big wedding. The big wedding may seem like a fairy tale come true, but it has worrying emotional and financial implications. The 'big wedding' lasts only a day but the bills will be with you for a long time, unless of course you have a healthy bank balance.

It is still customary for parents of Indian origin to foot the bill. It is estimated that the girl's parents can be out of pocket by £30 to £50 K depending upon their standing in the community. If questioned, people shrug their shoulders and say that it is a tradition, or they are doing it to 'save face' or they want their children to be well settled.

It can be a very stressful occasion though the marriage ceremony, whether religious or civil, is quite simple and inexpensive. In my view, it is the reception or celebrations which precede and follow the actual ceremony that engender stress. The only consolation is that Christmas comes every year and marriages on average happen three or four times in our lifetimes.

There are quite a few examples where people have plumped for simple marriages. I read in a newspaper that the bridegroom and his friends went to the wedding on their bicycles. The bridegroom brought his bride on his bicycle, even though he could have afforded to hire a limousine. Some people may find this odd, but others will see him as a trendsetter who didn't care two hoots for tradition or following others blindly.

If you want a lavish marriage, you may wish to discuss the following questions with your partner and/or family. If you are a businessman or businesswoman who wants to entertain your potential customers or to develop your network, then the questions do not apply to you.

1. Why do you want to spend unstintingly on your marriage celebrations?

2. Is it because of tradition or because you want to do it?

3. If it is because of tradition, how can you change it?

4.   Whom do you want to impress, and why?

5.   Have you considered changing the big wedding to a slightly smaller wedding and giving part of what you intend to spend to a charity so that you feel you have also done a good deed?

6.   If you are from an Indian background, have you considered the girl's perspective? **Put yourself in her parent's shoes and reflect on how you would feel if you had to foot the bill**

STRESS AT WORK

You can transform dissatisfaction at work into satisfaction and maintain your sanity. If you view work as something you have to do to sustain yourself, that is fine, but this way of thinking might make you unhappy or dissatisfied.

However, if you think of your work as an opportunity to do something good for society, then you will be viewing your work as something really worthwhile. You will then be ascribing a higher purpose to your work, and might become more industrious because it is a calling and not ordinary mundane work. Your willingness to undergo hardship will be greater, and obstacles will be overcome easily.

We are living in a culture of deadlines and the world is getting faster. Some of us work up to 12 to 14 hours a day. Some corner shops are open from eight in the morning to ten in the evening, seven days a week. We rush to meet so-and-so from such-and-such company or organisation, or the deadlines. We are always in a hurry, stuck in a rat race. We have allowed ourselves to get into that terrible habit of working for the sake of it, to impress our line managers, or our bosses, and perhaps our friends and underlings as well. If you ask most people who seem to be very busy, "What exactly do you do?" the answer is normally, "I am not sure." Quantity, as we all know, doesn't always translate into quality. What exactly are we busy for? I suspect that some of us are hurrying to an early grave.

Of course employers have a responsibility to determine how much work an employee can be reasonably expected to handle. I have seen donkeys overloaded with bricks, and oxen having to pull huge weights on bullock carts in developing countries. It is cruelty to the animal. Too much overload at a workplace shows lack of concern and lack of respect for the individual. If you are working in an environment that is not humane, which is driven by bigger profits and making more money, by all means you should try to change their manner of thinking. This type of environment creates the conditions for all kinds of inequities, unfairness and stress.

ATTITUDE TO WORK

An attitude is a way of thinking and feeling about someone or something. Attitude to work is the most important factor in achieving a sense of fulfilment. For some a job is only for earning money, but those who achieve real job satisfaction see their paid job as meaningful, having a higher purpose. They believe that they are making a contribution to society. Your attitude to work can have a profound effect on your job satisfaction and a sense of fulfilment. If one has a negative attitude to work, the individual can do some reflection and analysis to discover how the negative thoughts can be overcome. Each of us has the capacity to cultivate greater work satisfaction by transforming a job into a calling. If you still find the job boring, or you are not happy at the workplace in spite of your efforts to transform your negative thoughts and beliefs into more positive thinking, then you should look for another 'interesting' job.

A person could have very routine work that might not be challenging, and then in such cases the individual needs other sources of satisfaction and fulfilment. Such a person needs to have a life outside work, spending more time with family and friends. People doing routine repetitive work could cultivate friendships at work; they may not have an interesting or stimulating job, but can have an interesting life. Some people do voluntary work or provide service to their community that gives them satisfaction and fulfilment. In such cases their paid job is simply a means to earn their livelihood.

In *Achieving a Healthy Balanced Life!* I dwelt on the fact that we need a balanced life which pays attention to our physical well-being, to the spiritual dimension, to our social life, the mind and our emotional intelligence. We should earn our livelihood by honest means, so work is important to sustain us, but our life should not be centred round work only. A job which was exciting in the beginning may lose its charm after some time. Personal growth and continued development is essential to give us a sense of fulfilment.

Developing our physical fitness, paying attention to emotional needs and spiritual advancement and having a social life can be our primary source of satisfaction. One who trains regularly for physical fitness, prepares the body and mind for mental training and endeavours to find spiritual upliftment can return to work with renewed interest and energy

KNOW YOUR CALLING

The characteristic of a calling would be that we see our work as contributing to some greater good, serving others, and associated with some meaning. The concept of calling has to do with some higher purpose, the social good or welfare of others. At present I am very passionate about writing. I believe that it is my calling.

People make sense of others by labelling them, putting complex individuals in little pigeonholes. You are much bigger than a mere label. Your critics look at you from one angle, most probably at your weaknesses and your friends probably pay more attention to your positives. The trick is not to internalise any label which your friends, colleagues or enemies may want to stick on to you. Please find your own identity, understand and surface your own values and look at your work, your job or profession as a calling.

A research study showed that generally speaking in the West, some people view their work in one of three categories. Some people view their work as simply a job to earn money, and the weekly or monthly wage packet is their main motivation and interest. This attitude to work is understandable as we need money to sustain ourselves. People in the job market sometimes have a number of mouths to feed, and their primary interest in working would be to make sure that their dependants at least get three square meals a day. There are others who view their work as a career, and people in this second category focus on career development, promotion, going up the ladder advancement, self and professional development. There are some people who view their work as a calling or a vocation. In this third category, people have an inward feeling and regard their employment as requiring dedication.

It is said that Prince Harry went to Afghanistan as a party boy and transformed his image in ten weeks. Seeing action with Blues and Royals in Helmand fulfilled his dream, and obviously the young prince found his vocation. Whilst fighting in Afghanistan, the young prince like other soldiers experienced freezing cold nights, boiling days, bland rations—and the fear. But his interviews indicate that he seems to have relished every moment of it. He preferred being 'with the lads' and 'mucking in' to living in England in a palace. His comments about army life—"It could be the best thing in the world, and the best job you could wish for"—"clearly sum up why it is a vocation for him.

After leaving university, Prince Harry's life was aimless. Entry into the Royal Military Academy, Sandhurst, gave direction to his life, and fighting for his country helped him to find his vocation as a soldier.

ENERGY-DRAINING WORRIES

Our past experiences influence our current behaviour. We think about our past glories and the failures. When we sit with our friends, most of the time is spent on regurgitating old stories, anecdotes and incidents. We live in the past though the past is not our future. Some of us have drawn very negative lessons from our experiences and we dwell in negativity.

Most of the blocks that people experience come from negative self-talk and negative beliefs. Some of us wrongly think that we are our acts, and if we have failed at something in the past, we think we will not succeed in the future. Thoughts such as, *I am not good enough, I am not that disciplined or I am not that smart*—all stand in the way of improvement. So we worry that we will not succeed in the future.

The next piece headed 'Enhanced Insight' aims to help you in the process of having a better appraisal or raised self-awareness.

ENHANCED INSIGHT

By focussing your mind on the experience, your aim is to gain deeper insight into your own way of working, your personality and your habits. If the appraisal is not done with an open mind, you may find yourself justifying your actions rather than learning from the experience. The experience will not be presenting any lessons to you then. You need to notice if you are trying to repress feelings without acknowledging them and responding wisely.

No doubt some tragedies like earthquakes, floods and fatalities through some senseless wars do not seem to have a worthwhile purpose. Many lives are lost; what took years to build is destroyed in minutes and people feel devastated. Some people, though, who are not crushed by such tragic events grow through such suffering and loss.

As regards our normal experiences, everything happens for a reason. We may not see it or appreciate it, but whatever happens in our lives is meant to help us grow into who we are meant to be or to help us to move forward on our journey. So why not choose to believe that the experience is a blessing in disguise, and choose to find positives in the experience or the lessons presented to you? If you don't reflect with an open mind, or do it mechanically, it is likely that the same mistakes will be repeated and the same results will be produced. Proper concentration is that which unifies the heart and mind. Reflecting in this way enables you to develop a skilful approach to a deeper insight.

The Learning Process

- **Experience:** The experience may be Reactive—something happened to you, or Proactive—an experience which you deliberately chose to have.

- **Reflection:** A non-judgemental look at what happened. The reflection can be done quite quickly, or we can take time to review the whole experience.

- **Conclusion:** Draw conclusions from the thoughts and any notes made at the reflection stage to identify the lessons learnt.

- **Plan:** Plan to test the lessons learnt at the conclusion stage, so that they can be related and applied to similar situations in the future.

HONOUR CODE

We still hear of honour killings and honour beatings. People still kill each other because they perceive that the other person has not shown them enough respect or has dishonoured them. Some extreme forms of honour codes still exist in some communities. An honour code is one in which the greatest punishment is shame, and revenge is a duty

Practically each culture, each community has tales which inculcated an ideal manhood. In the past and up to a large extent even today people use physical and mental endowments to the utmost to earn the applause of their comrades. Aspiring heroes were expected to seek opportunities to display courage and prowess—best of all in the teeth of danger. Fitness and strength of body, fortitude, courage and boldness were the qualities sought after, and made a warrior or a hunter. Recipients of the Victoria Cross get lots of publicity and admiration from the public not only in England but perhaps all over the world. Some wealthy collectors are prepared to pay huge sums of money to buy the decoration awarded for 'conspicuous bravery' in the armed forces.

Courage, bravery generosity, mercy, fairness are virtues which bring happiness to their possessors and others. They are very useful in the promotion of good fellowship. Does adherence to old honour codes serve any purpose in this age? Violence spawns violence and honour killings can last many generations. Some people have the memory of an elephant and they never forget. I have heard some people say that they will never sleep peacefully till revenge has been exacted. I wonder what type of life they lead, thinking of revenge all the time? Certainly it is not a peaceful one, as the mind is focused on revenge which involves harming or killing the other party.

The old rule of revenge and feud is not necessary any more, certainly not in advanced countries. It has been replaced by a due process of law before a civil court. I do not think any one can have real peace of mind after harming or murdering another human being.

In some communities, women still do not have any status or liberties. Young girls are forced to marry their parent's choice and are abused in their in-laws' homes. They are deeply unhappy, but are told to be mindful of their family name and stop complaining. The family name or honour matters more than anything: it is given precedence over the happiness of their own flesh and blood. Some girls do not accept the oppression and fight back, but others bear it and carry themselves around like whipped dogs. Their spirit is broken. One wonders how the parents can have even a modicum of happiness and can be tranquil when their daughters are living in an unsavoury environment.

Guru Nanak put it very elegantly when he said:

> *It is by women that we are conceived;*
> *And from them that we are born;*
> *It is with them that we are betrothed and married;*
> *It is the women we befriend and it is they who keep the race going;*
> *When one woman dies, we seek another.*
> *It is with women that we become established in society.*
> *Why should women be called inferior when they give birth to great men?*

We naturally like the recognition our community gives in return for services rendered. In England there was a huge inquiry into the cash-for-honours affair. Scotland Yard's inquiry lasted more than 15 months after it emerged that secret loans had been given to a political party before the 2005 general election and some lenders had been nominated for peerages.

Honour is nobleness of mind, doing what is right. If your understanding of honour is different please consider the following questions:

Some questions to think about—and answer:

- What is your definition of 'honour'?

- What is honourable about harming or killing somebody?

- If you harm somebody and get incarcerated in prison for years, is the action 'honourable' or foolish?

MEDITATION: AWARENESS OF THE BODY

We do get tensed up when stressed, but are not always aware of it. The palms may have moisture, the pulse may be fast, the chest tightening up, but we ignore the signs.

Use a posture that will keep your back straight without strain. Most of us tend to hunch our shoulders when sitting down. If you have a tendency unconsciously to do that, imagine that someone is gently pushing between the shoulder blades, while keeping the muscles relaxed. If you are stooping forward, please do straighten the spine. If you decide to sit in a cross-legged position, (Sukh Aasan), keep the arms light and held back against the stomach or on the knees. Sukh Aasan is the most popular position as it is comfortable. 'Sukh' means comfort in Punjabi, Hindi and Urdu. Take your time and get the right balance.

Breathe gently, and move your attention systematically from the crown of your head down over the whole body. Notice the sensations as you move your attention. Notice the moisture of the palms. Relax any tensions, particularly in the face, neck and hands. Consciously put aside all the memories and expectations of tomorrow and keep your attention on noticing the sensations and relaxing the tensions. Allow the eyelids to close. You can meditate on your breath, maintaining your attention at one point—nostrils, if you feel overwhelmed by sensations. Breath has a tranquillising quality if you don't force it.

If you find other thoughts drifting in, memories, things to be done or other pressures, or even doubts if you are doing the right thing, bring your attention to your body. Use the body as an anchor for a wandering mind.

VARIATION OF THE POSTURE

If you find it difficult to sit in the cross-legged position—called Sukh Aasan in Yoga—you can try meditation (mokuso—in the Japanese language) while sitting on the knees (seiza position) like the Japanese monks and martial artists.

1. From the standing position, draw the left foot to the rear.

2. Kneel down on the left knee, and place it (the left knee) next to the heel of the right foot.

3. Kneel down with the right knee parallel to the left knee. The knees are separated by two fists' width.

4. Place the right foot on the sole of the left foot. Some instructors ask you to place the big toe of the right foot on the big toe of the left foot.

5. In Yoga it is called Vajran Aasan, though the feet are not crossed.

6. Release tension from the body, keep the back straight and keep the hands on the thighs.

7. Practise meditation as described above.

DEEP BREATHNG

Everyone breathes, but most people are what Kay Porter calls 'thoracic' or chest breathers in *The Mental Athlete*. In our everyday breathing, we inhale through the nose, and then the air goes to the throat, windpipe and into the lungs. The oxygen passes into the blood, and the body's tissues constantly take up oxygen from the blood and release carbon dioxide back into the blood. Carbon dioxide is a waste gas that must be removed by the lungs via the blood.

When we are under stress, our muscles tighten, the heart beats more rapidly and breathing becomes fast and shallow. Breathing deeply when stressed is one of the most valuable techniques one can learn for calming, focusing and energizing. As you breathe deeply, you relax your emotions and let go of your body tensions.

There are four basic types of belly breathing:

1. Inhale very slowly and deeply, exhale slowly and completely.

2. Inhale very slowly and deeply, exhale quickly.

3. Inhale quickly, exhale slowly and completely.

4. Inhale quickly, exhale quickly.

For this deep breathing exercise, please use type 1 of breathing, i.e. inhale very slowly and deeply, exhale slowly and completely. Stand with both the feet parallel to each other and the toes turned inwards with the arms in front, bent at the elbows, so that the lower arms are parallel to the ground or floor. The fists can be clenched with the fingers pointing upwards or the hands can be open with the fingers pointing in front. Bend the knees and thighs inwards.

When you breathe in, imagine a stream of air entering your body through the nose and following a path up and around the body, down the neck to be concentrated into a tight ball at a point just below the navel as you complete the inhalation of the breath. When exhaling, the air rises from the point under the navel, to the solar plexus to the throat and out slowly from the mouth.

The eyes look straight ahead with the chin drawn in slightly. When inhaling and exhaling ensure that the chest is open, the abdominal muscles tightened and the back is straight. Other things to do:

• Tense the thigh muscles.

• Tighten the buttock muscles.

• Bend the knees.

• Grip the floor with the toes and soles of the feet as if you are trying to root yourself to the ground.

• Keep the muscles tensed throughout the performance.

After you have practised the abdominal breathing over a period of time, you will be able to concentrate all your power in your breathing. This accomplishment, I believe, will help you to deal with stress situations in a much calmer manner,

NOTE: This technique is a simplified version of a Kata—a formal sequence of practice exercises and movements from Goju Ryu karate. The Sanchin Kata incorporates a number of other movements which I have intentionally left out. I learnt the Kata when I was young and still practise it practically every day.

6

Feelings And Emotions

BEING IN TOUCH WITH OUR FEELINGS

The movements of expression on the face and body, whatever their origin may have been, are by themselves of much importance for our welfare. They serve as the first means of communication between the mother and her offspring. Her smile of approval encourages the child on the right path and her frown of disapproval discourages the infant from pursuing a certain action. The expressions give vividness and energy to our spoken words. They reveal the thoughts and intentions of others more truly than do words, which may be falsified.

In everyday life, we think that to some extent we can tell how our friends or near ones are feeling. In doing so, we note facial expression, posture, tone of voice, physiological changes, rate or speed of movement, and early actions. All the changes are noted in reference to the situations in which they occur. The stronger the feeling being experienced by our companion, and especially in a clear situation, the more confident we feel that we can identify what is going on with the individual.

Langer notes that 'feel' is a verb, and to say that what is felt is a feeling may be deceptive: 'the phenomenon usually described as "a feeling" is deceptive.' What is felt is a process; it could be an emotion, or sensation—within the organism. Her explanation is that 'Being felt' is a phase of the process itself.

By 'phase' Langer means one of the many modes in which something may appear without anything having been added or subtracted from it. She considers the heating or cooling of iron to illustrate her point:

'When iron is heated to a critical degree it becomes red; yet its redness is not a new entity which must have gone somewhere else when it is no longer in the iron. It was a phase of the iron itself, at high temperature.'

The question then is how the phase of being felt is attained and how the process can be controlled. Sensory data regarding the environmental events reaches the organism via its sense organs. It can also reach the organism from its internal states. Once their general relevance is determined, some sequence of behaviour, especially reflex actions or fixed actions, proceed without much further action.

The individual, who feels what is felt, is a reflection of how he/she is appraising the situation and what types of behaviour are from time-to-time being activated by him/her. Thus to the individual, the feelings provide a monitoring service or a thermometer of his/her physiological state. This is why it is important to be in touch with your feelings. A person who has insight into his/her feelings can therefore acknowledge that he/she is angry with his/her life partner or is still grieving for his/her father. Such an individual is mindful of his/her feelings or emotions. Emotions are strong mental feelings such as love or fear. When we say that I am feeling amorous, angry or afraid, these words denote emotions.

When we are angry with someone, it is unlikely that we do what we are motivated to do. If one is angry with one's partner, one is unlikely to attack him/her. Feelings tell us ways in which a situation is being appraised. Feelings can activate behavioural systems and can be monitored too. A person who has insight can note the feelings and the process that follows. If he/she is angry with him/her, then he/she needs to be mindful of behavioural systems that are being communicated by noting the behaviour and what he/she says. Similarly if one is overwhelmed by jealousy, then the individual needs to be aware how he/she reacts to the person, and his/her verbal communication with the other party who has given rise to the feeling.

The language of feeling is an indispensable vehicle for talking about ways in which a situation is appraised, about behavioural systems in a state of activation, and whether activation is leading to overt behaviour. Your sense of what is right or wrong plays a strong part in putting a stop to acting on your impulses, as because of INHIBITION, the behaviour activated remains undeveloped or in an initial stage.

USEFUL TIPS

• If you feel uncomfortable when you consider a possible future, your discomfort will not disappear if you choose it.

• When you base your decisions on external considerations and ignore your feelings, you are likely to create painful experiences.

• If you hate somebody ten times a day, confront the feeling ten times a day.

• If you are conscious of what you are feeling and have the courage to confront the irrational feelings rather than acting in fear or irresponsibly, you are likely to make rational choices and develop inner strength.

COMPASSION

Leaders whose positions endure are those who are the most compassionate (Ancient Chinese sage—Lao Tzu)

It is said that one hot day when Gautama Buddha was about to travel from one village to another, one of his disciples by the name of Anand filled the begging bowl with water as the other village was quite far. On the way, Gautama Buddha asked for the begging bowl and poured all the water on a withering plant. Anand told Gautama Buddha that he had carried the water to quench their thirst. Gautama Buddha replied that when we feel thirsty, we shall see what can be done, but the plant is dying now.

Kindness and compassion originate from the same source of goodwill. Kindness and compassion broaden the mind to look at issues or things beyond the purely personal perspective. If we are not always trying to make things go the way we want them to, and instead are more accepting of ourselves and others as they are, compassion arises by itself.

We often think that compassion is something that we have for other people, but the biggest favour we can do to ourselves is to develop compassion for ourselves. Charity begins at home. Self-compassion allows you to forge ahead when everything around you seems to be on the verge of collapse.

When we feel the pain that we can't bear to feel, or we can't face, instead of running away from it, or blaming the other party, or doing something against the other, just sit down and feel it as it is. It is perfectly in order to feel miserable, to feel the fear, to feel the despair, or whatever we are feeling. Then you can recognise how you are judging the situation, your appraisal, and you can change or modify the way you are looking at the situation.

We think that certain feelings will be permanent; they will stay with us forever. No thought or feeling stays with us for long. But once we accept the feeling as it is, somehow in that space of acceptance, there is a release also. When we allow ourselves to feel exactly what we are feeling, there is a moment of release as we recognise that the feelings pass because they are not being held; they are being let go of. We are not fixing them through resisting, or struggling, or judging. Feelings never stay the same.

We create stories around a moment of feeling, and suffer a lot of pain and pressure. We never find happiness, because we do not have a knack for looking under the surface of initial reactivity. Our reactions are conditioned, and we respond the same way to similar situations. When we are unhappy, we need to recognise that it has a cause, and that cause can be seen here and now, in our own current experience. It doesn't have to be traced back in memory, in time. We think the cause could be what someone said, or did, things that were so hurtful. We could be saying: 'I am getting what I don't want i.e. criticism or disapproval and not getting what I want' i.e. praise or appreciation—but ask yourself: 'What is the present cause in the present moment?' Quite often we will find that it is in our relationship to the presently arising feeling, the way we struggle with it. As long as we are alive, there will always be people who are going to annoy us, miff us one way or the other. We can't have everything we want, and everything will never be done 'my way'. If we are mindful, we can be in control and not allow others to take away our tranquillity or peace of mind.

We find a sense of freedom coming through, not clinging, allowing life to flow at will, in tune with nature. There is greater freedom to choose how to respond rather than react automatically, and a greater clarity of mind to reflect upon situations.

We can choose to act or not to act according to how we understand the situation, or appraise the situation, and as tolerance and a certain kind of courage and compassion grow, we find that our disposition is much more of not wanting to harm or hurt others or ourselves. One becomes more sensitive to what's wholesome, what's worth developing—not only for ourselves but for all those we're involved with in our lives. It all starts with a willingness to feel what we feel, to know what we think, and to recognise how our thoughts affect our feelings and how judgement arises.

USEFUL HINTS

- Compassion creates co-operation.

- Compassion means to accept one another in spite of differences.

- When you treat others with compassion, they become more cooperative.

- Subordinates who experience compassion are more willing to take risks.

- Subordinates who are chastised in front of others, work with fear of making a mistake.

- "Compassion is the inner perspective that enables you to empathise with another, to look at a situation from that person's point of view." (Jerry Lynch)

- Your compassion will permeate your whole family, or your 'team'. They will become compassionate with one another, forgive one another and grow together through setbacks and difficult times.

WHAT CAN YOU DO TO OVERCOME NEGATIVE FEELINGS?

SUGGESTIONS

There is nothing wrong about feeling our feelings, touching our pain, and at the same time understanding the truth of the way things are. It is only when we are aware of them, that we can accept the grief, the pain or the loss.

To be aware of your feelings requires a careful approach. This can be done by:

- Careful attention to how we experience ourselves at present—this moment.

- How do you experience others?

- If it is ill-will or malevolence which is being experienced, practise kindliness to the other person. Be benign, and look at the good qualities of the other person. It is crucial to remember to separate behaviours from the person.

- By taking responsibility for what we feel, taking responsibility for our actions and speech, we build the foundation of the path to inner strength.

- This does not mean that we have to like everybody, but we need to control our mind from lingering in states of negativity or aversion towards others.

- **Treat others as you would like to be treated.**

- If lust or greed is being experienced, use your intelligence in choosing a technique suitable to bring about and support a state of calmness and inner tranquillity. An analytical approach can often be effective in inducing a sense of neutrality or disinterest.

- It is not just a matter of negative feelings being removed. Try to make it certain that they have been replaced by an enduring sense of calm, peacefulness, hope and inner strength.

- Handling situations involves learning to use your cognitive ability to respond on a level above the emotions of the specific situation.

- Instead of going off the handle, use a more cerebral, rational approach.

- Promise yourself: 'I refuse to give any person or situation permission to distract me from my ethics, my **values**, which I hold to be true.'

EMOTIONS

For every waking hour, emotions and feelings are with us, sloshing around our heads, effecting powerful changes in us, making our hearts beat faster, or miss a beat; hands sweat or fists clench, shoulders getting tensed up, or butterflies in the stomach. Emotions both motivate and disable every human on the planet with rage, guilt, disappointment, worry, bafflement, regret, or cheerfulness and determination.

According to ancient Chinese philosophy, there are only five basic emotions: Anger, fear, grief, love, and jealousy. Robert Plutchnik, one of the most influential persons in the field of emotions, identifies eight human emotions: Anger, Fear, Sadness, Disgust, Surprise, Curiosity, Acceptance and Joy. Some modern thinkers consider that there are many more emotions than the above eight. Perhaps you can think of some which are relevant to you.

KEEPING YOUR COOL

Anger controlled is strength.
Don't waste anger.
Channel it.

We all know that it is a waste of time and energy to lose our temper. We damage relationships or friendships in anger, and then expend considerable energy and effort to repair the damage done in the heat of the moment.

When somebody 'pushes a button', we do things in our anger such as shout, berate and rant. We do not want to create damage, but part of the personality that is frustrated, angry, or resentful wants to punish the perceived wrongdoer. We become righteous and rigid; we don't want to listen to the other person but want to be heard. We want to impose our desires, our wishes on the other party. We may want to have a meaningful relationship, a constructive discussion, but when ANGRY, or resentful, the real intention is lost.

As far as your own health is concerned, research shows that a person's blood pressure goes up when angry, and that it keeps rising seven days later if the cause of the anger is remembered. We presume that blood pressure would return to normal once an argument was finished, but researchers from the University of California and Columbia University, found that 'even after a week, there is no sign of any reduction of the effect'. Anger has been linked to heart disease and research has suggested that hardening of arteries occurs faster in people who score highly in hostility and anger tests.

Aristotle saw anger as an emotion capable of great power and good effect if wisely directed. If it is 'to fly into a passion' he remarked, anyone can do that; 'but to be angry with the right person to the right extent, at the right time, in the right way with the right aim, that is not easy'. He thought that knowing how to be appropriately angry is an essential part of the moral life—provided that it does not overthrow reason and become merely destructive in consequence.

If you are conscious of your values, most probably you would like to be firm and fair which requires you to model composure during difficult times. Your aim when delivering or receiving a negative message is to defuse anger and hostility and make the interaction cordial or at least less anxious.

To defuse a volatile situation, we need to trust our innate wisdom. You do not have to be a slave to your instincts; you can keep your control by being flexible. Flexibility and humour are effective tools for resolving conflict. We can always blend and bend rather than fight with might. Your personal strength and power as a person will increase with your ability to be flexible. It is always very tempting to 'teach others a lesson', by using force, or psychological pressure, but by going head to head you run the risk of creating a negative and harsh environment in which nobody is really the winner. When one subdues another with physical force, or threats, one loses the moral high ground.

USEFUL HINTS

• When you are angry, you may feel overwhelmed and out of control. Remember that you are not these feelings; they are simply things that you do and feel.

• Decide if you want to be controlled by that part of your personality that is angry or resentful. If not, say to yourself: "I have the ability to act differently."

• Often anger is a result of feelings of resentment or frustration that you experience. But resentment binds you, keeps you down; you blame others, feel trapped and believe you are a victim.

• Anger is a natural process, one to be observed and expressed appropriately. Be aware of it.

• Acknowledge your anger and the associated feelings.

• Breathe to calm yourself—deep breaths, down to your solar plexus and out slowly.

• Relax your shoulders, neck and abdomen. You can do some shoulder exercises like rotating the shoulders or 'shrugging' (raising the shoulders and rotating them clockwise first and then anticlockwise).

How to Manage your Anger

Awareness of the way things are

As human beings, we have a mind that can reflect and observe. You can be aware whether you are happy or unhappy. If you are angry, you can observe the anger, the frustration and the confusion in your mind. When you sit down and feel upset, through being self-aware you know it. You might hate it, succumb to your anger and just blindly react to it, but with patience you can observe that this is a temporary changing condition, of confusion, anger, or hatred. An animal cannot reflect on it; when it is angry, it is completely lost in it. You observe the impulse, the way it is, and know that it is a temporary and changing condition. We need to understand that whatever is happening in our life, misery, ugliness, anger, pain or pleasure, happiness—are impermanent conditions.

Let me narrate an incident so as to explain how the technique can be used in real life. A close relative of mine (let us call him X) was insulted by the host (let us call her Y) at a funeral. I thought that it was wrong of Y to ask X to leave and not to participate in the ceremony because of some previous differences. X had travelled a long distance and had spent a considerable amount of money to travel to the place. The incident took root in my mind and I became angrier and angrier with Y. I started analysing the whole episode and the analysis of course was not dispassionate. The more I thought about it, the more resentful and furious I became, because I believed that it is wrong to insult a person who has come to your place. One has got to be courteous to a guest, whatever his or her shortcomings. I started digging out all Y's negative aspects, and cursed myself for not walking out with X.

I even started looking into the future and wondered whether the incident would affect my relations with X as I had encouraged him to be there. In short, I was nurturing my anger. The more I thought about it, the more hatred I was developing for Y. My anger was overwhelming, and I was not managing it properly. There was no self-mastery or temperance, and I was allowing it to affect my tranquillity.

1. MYOPIC VIEW

When we have a negative experience, we believe that it will not go away; it is permanent, though the reality is that everything in this world is impermanent. We also personalize it, in the sense that we think the experience always happens to 'me only', whereas others may be affected by the same experience or have similar or even worse negative experiences all the time. We also tend to think in terms of an incident developing into a catastrophe and envisage a disastrous end.

I could not get rid of the emotions even though I tried to confront them. I was becoming a hostage to them. All the time my thinking was: 'The host should not have done this, or done that.' I was also thinking of a catastrophic outcome rather than being rational and looking at how to solve the problem itself. I was wondering about my future with my relative and whether I had damaged my relationship with him forever. Could I really rebuild it? In short, I was getting attached to the emotion, carrying it around in my mind and not looking for a safe harbour to put down my burden.

So if we look at the situation, my belief system was playing havoc with my tranquillity. The belief was that the host should have been more understanding, more magnanimous, and not petty in feelings and conduct. My beliefs are:

1. If a person comes to your house, you should appreciate that the guest has put differences to one side to be present at the occasion.

2. Even if Y and her family did not want him to attend the funeral, he should have been forewarned, or at least given a hint that he was not welcome at the solemn occasion.

3. If it is possible, one should attend the funeral of an old friend or relative to pay one's respects.

We may find our belief system helpful at times, but we have to find ways to cope inwardly when confronting a perceived unfairness. Instead of developing frustration or hatred, we need to train our minds to remain calm. To remain calm in such situations, **we can use our human intelligence to analyse the situation and see it from a different perspective.**

2. WIDER PERSPECTIVE

Learn to read reality with different eyes and you will learn the art of remaining peaceful and happy.

When we are angry, we tend to think in black and white terms only. But every thing in life is relative. So based on this reality, one can cultivate a wider perspective of the situation and try to see it from different angles. If for example, one is sacked from a workplace, it could be because of the economy or in the public sector—cuts by the government. The grieved party does not have to hold a grudge against the boss and try to harm him or her.

In the abovementioned instance, **I was not** looking at the situation from Y's perspective; I had to put myself in the family's shoes. The family were in bereavement and possibly did not want to add to their sorrow by accommodating somebody they had differences with. It is possible that they were not able to comprehend the consequences of their actions because of their own suffering and loss. Somebody with strong empathic skills, or proficiency in Emotional Intelligence, might come up with any number of benign reasons for a hostile attitude.

3. FREEING THE HEART

If we meet the present moment with mindfulness and wise reflection, we can surrender our feelings and emotions, free our heart, and receive the next moment with purity of mind. When we feel down or depressed or angry, it's only one mental state—and do we want to perpetuate such a state for a lifetime? So we have an option: we can stay angry, depressed or miserable which is the realm of hell, or stay in a state of peace that comes from wisdom. When people feel love towards us we feel peaceful and calmer. This is what we can do to ourselves too; cultivate kindness and infinite patience towards ourselves. When one is angry, the mind dwells upon negative aspects of oneself and others. When I was angry, I was not kind to myself, but judgemental. I was looking too much into the future, as to what might happen. We need to remind ourselves to remain mindful; it is an endless refrain, mindful, mindful. The practice of awareness is always in the present moment.

4. CHOOSE YOUR RESPONSE

- Deliberately analyse whether responding with anger and hatred will benefit or harm us in the near future and in the long run. **Be compassionate to yourself.**

- Reflect on whether responding with anger or revulsion brings a happier or more peaceful state of mind or if the emotions we are experiencing serve to make us miserable, frustrated and dissatisfied.

- Relate to a past experience, think about the effect which such emotions had on your physical health and emotional state.

- Think how the others responded to you when you were angry or full of revulsion.

- Did your behaviour or actions help you to have a better relationship or did they damage the relationship?

- Think deeply whether it is worth responding with hostility or is it better to discuss the matter calmly and confidently.

- How beneficial will be the positive emotions like tolerance and contentment in resolving the issue or conflict?

So we do not have to react impetuously or automatically to any provocation—we have the freedom to choose our response. You can act in conformity with your objectives, and your principles. Kant's most famous imperative is: "Act in such a way that you always treat humanity, whether in your own person or in the person of any other, never simply as a means, but always at the same time as an end."

COMPLAINING

When not satisfied with a service, or when harbouring resentment towards a friend, family or a rival, one can be angry, fuming, vengeful and at times inarticulate with rage. Some people bad mouth, shout, scream and rant to give vent to their feelings. Some do not vent their feelings—they may be the strong 'anger in' types. I have dealt with quite a few offenders whose focus was not on making themselves better, but in punishing the people who have wronged them. Their anger is cold, calculating, not impulsive but vengeful. It has more to do with sadistic punishment than restorative justice.

If we are not satisfied with a service, I believe that we should complain. Some people do not complain. Perhaps they believe that it does no good. So long as one **lets go** of the anger, does not harbour a grudge or resentment, it is fine, it is healthiest. Perhaps they subscribe to the maxim that, 'It is human to err and divine to forgive.'

On the other hand, there are many people who are referred to as 'conflict avoiders'. They bottle their anger and avoid conflict at all costs. They are terrified of confrontations; perhaps they are good at placation but cannot be seen as assertive. These people may believe anger is bad and do not want to express it. They see anger as being out of control of their emotions, which is not acceptable to them. Such a belief system often results in those adhering to it in dissociating from their emotions and true feelings and eventually may lead to illness.

If you have a genuine complaint or grievance against somebody, remember that we are all human beings. If you are self-aware, you will be conscious of all the painful emotions and the reactions that are arising. Instead of making unconscious choices, you decide what the best course of action is. You take control of your decisions just like a driver takes control of a car. You are not on autopilot, you decide upon the method to deal with the situation.

You may not be satisfied with a service you have received; your expectations have not been met, but you recognise that we are all interdependent, and we can influence another's attitude and make a difference by modelling the correct response. We all have the capacity to relate to each other with warmth and understanding

When we are in conflict with another, one is most likely to feel fear or hostility rather than to think of the other person as another human being, as worthy of your compassion as anyone else. When we cultivate deep compassion, ideally it should be directed toward everyone equally. According to the Dalai Lama, 'that's genuine compassion, universal compassion.'

COPING WITH A LOSS AND DESPAIR

Uncertainty and change are very much part of the modern way of living. People lose their friends, relationships break up, and marriages end up in divorce. In the current economy, there is no certainty with regard to employment. So in view of prevailing circumstances, there may be some situations where we have some control, but in others we have very little. Let us deal with employment, to explore how an individual can deal with the loss of a job.

Some people acknowledge that they have a job one day, and may not be working at the same workplace the next day. They study the trends; have the necessary knowledge about the global economy and the local conditions. If there is some complaint about their personal competence, they take the necessary steps to enhance their skills so that the employers do not have cause to fire them. They rehearse mentally how they will respond when the bad news comes. When it happens, they are not surprised, but accept it. They may not have control over the situation, but they have control over their attitude, in the way they take in the news.

Some feel devastated after hearing that they have lost the job. They look at the loss in pervasive or catastrophic terms—'I will never get another job!' Another individual may look at the loss of a job as an opportunity to try new things, become self-employed, get some training or qualifications and then enter the job market. It is our attitude that decides more than any other factor. When there is a stimulus, we have a choice as to how to respond to it. We can choose the negative way and stagnate or we can choose the positive or proactive way. Pro-active people concentrate on what is possible rather than what is immovable at that particular time.

Those with a strong religious belief say that it is God's will and something good will come out of it. Such a belief is comforting. It will ease the psychological effect and reduce the mental agony. People who do not have a religion will probably say that such an attitude can be fatalistic, that what has happened was destined to happen, and that it was inevitable. The belief that something good will come out of it does not mean that the person accepts the situation with resignation, and helplessness, but accepts it philosophically and begins to explore other avenues. The teachings and tenets of the religion, and the values being held by the person will also come into play.

One of the three main principles of Sikhism is to earn one's livelihood by honest means. Honesty also may be one of your values. So a person with such a belief system will strive to secure another job and not blame others for the misfortune.

I know of some people who love their job, but visualize how they will cope if they are pushed.

VISUALIZATION

To be disciplined in body, mind and spirit, people practise meditation and visualization. People renew themselves through meditation, they make time to practise meditation on a regular basis, and gradually, it becomes a habit.

Athletes and sportspeople use Visualization to master certain techniques prior to their competitions. They rehearse in their minds each and every step they are going to take in a competition or when mastering a skill.

VISUALIZATION (1)—BEING IN CONTROL

In a relaxed state, with your eyes closed, imagine the angry party coming at you with a verbal barrage. Notice the body language or non-verbal communication, the anger, and the insensitivity. Think calmly how you will respond calmly to the attack. Separate the person from the behaviour, accept the person; she may be a terrific person who is merely upset at present. Consider handling the situation by being open about it rather than tensing your body. Feel the calmness, the sense of power in that you are in control rather than being controlled by the other person.

You are choosing your response rather than reacting automatically. You choose to believe and say to yourself, "Nobody can make me angry."

You may wish to follow the following procedure first when visualizing and then in real interaction to defuse the anger:

1. Let the person talk, to get it all out.

2. Listen attentively

3. Express your feelings about being attacked—verbal onslaught.

4. See yourself expressing your views clearly, in a calm yet firm manner. **You are calm, controlled and collected.**

5. **Calm is patience. Calm speaks quiet and slow. It rules with the head, not with the heart.**

6. **Calm acts with caution and intelligence.**

7. Know that you have maintained your respect and the other person's dignity …

8. Go for a Win-Win outcome.

During the actual interaction, don't partially listen as you counter attack. Give your full attention instead. Try genuinely to understand and empathise with her position. Ask yourself, 'What is the person feeling right now?' I like Stephen Fry's advice in *Seven Habits of Highly Effective People*—'Seek to Understand Before Being Understood.' It is very tempting to interrupt, but hold onto what you want to say. Let the other person fully explain herself, and then express your feelings later.

Address the concern in a positive way. Ask the other person, "Now that we are clear on this, what can you suggest that can be done to help us both get what we want?" Even if the problem is not solved, anger will be dissipated up to a large extent, and the other party will walk away with a sense of dignity and self-esteem.

VISUALIZATION (2)—AT PEACE WITH THE WORLD

Meditation clears the mind and you can visualize your performance or your behaviour. Visualization can help you to create the person you want to be, a new you. If you want to be cool, calm and collected, try the following exercise:

Visualize yourself at peace with the world. In your visualization see yourself calm even when everyone around you is rushing like mad. See how undisturbed you are, at peace, how you embody sanity and tranquillity. Nothing can disturb your peace—you are unflappable whatever the circumstances. You are a model of harmony to others. Feel the calmness pervading your whole body.

VISUALIZATION (3)—DEALING WITH DIFFICULT PEOPLE

Sometimes we are nervous about interacting with a person who is perceived to be 'difficult', or a situation which could escalate into a confrontational or stressful one. Some people fear facing such situations, but if fear is controlled, it adds caution to courage. Preparation is imperative before the encounter if we want to have a positive outcome. Visualization can go a long way in helping you to achieve a 'win-win' outcome, rather than a negative or 'win-lose' situation or 'lose-win' result.

The beginning of the visualization should include focusing on your end goal and the outcome you want to achieve. The middle part may include the reaction of the other party and those around you. This part should consist of the interaction itself, everything you say, your strategy, your thoughts, feelings, your posture, tone of voice, body language or non-verbal communication. The final part encompasses all that is likely to happen, and you coming out with your dignity intact, and the other party feeling that they have been listened to and their respect maintained.

In the visualization, include as many senses as you can, and give yourself time to see, hear and feel what is likely to happen. See it all clearly and completely—as you want the interaction to proceed. Experience it exactly as you want it to be in reality. Focus on your thoughts, your words, and how you are going to say them, your actions and the responses from the other party.

With the proper preparation or visualization, **right thoughts and right actions,** there is no doubt that you will achieve the right outcome, which is a 'win-win' outcome.

BREATHING

One popular trick that many people use to remain calm is to take three breaths before speaking. You do not have to make it obvious that you are taking the breaths; it can be done discreetly. This will relax you. If you do lose your temper, do not hesitate to apologise, though in some circumstances it may be the most difficult thing to do. It is an appropriate way to bounce back and be calm, controlled and collected again.

I must mention here that at a 'Keep your Cool' course some participants did point out that taking deep breaths when somebody is shouting at you is not very practical.

Sometimes a joke or laughing can defuse a situation as:

> *Laughter knows no language.*
> *Laughter sails you through*
> *Good times and bad.*

THOUGHTS

> *Sow a thought, reap an action,*
> *Sow an action, reap a habit,*
> *Sow a habit, reap a trait,*
> *Sow a trait, reap a character,*
> *Sow a character, reap a destiny.*

Thoughts and actions are closely linked. Our actions stem from the seeds planted in the minds. But we are more than our thoughts, and nobody is punished for what one thinks. If we are mindful, negative thoughts can be replaced with positive ones. Thoughts which make us ill at ease can be substituted with more rational ones which restore our personal peace. You can separate the self from the thoughts.

If we continue to behave in the same way, take the same actions that we are used to, we will continue to produce the same results or the same consequences. If we want new and different results, then we have to think differently and take different actions. We reap what we sow. Imagine that you are a gardener or a farmer and it is planting time. Take some time to think about what seeds of action you can plant today to ensure a beautiful and exciting harvest in the coming months.

The energy we are devoting to plant what we want in the coming months could be to achieve tranquillity in our lives. Ask yourself:

- What would my peace with myself and peace with the world look like?

- How would I feel?

- What will be my thoughts?

If you intend to decrease the conflict and strengthen the bond with your spouse in the coming months, ask yourself again, "What do I need to do to turn a difficult relationship into a more loving one? What seeds of action do I need to plant today?

> *"The highest possible stage in moral culture is when we recognise that we ought to control our thoughts."*
>
> **—(The Descent of Man.)**

7

Mindfulness

With mindfulness, we can refrain from entertaining unpleasant thoughts. If some individuals are not nice to us, we do not have to be vindictive, have a desire to hurt them or 'finish' them. Even though we might not like them, we can still be kind and charitable to them. You can choose not to dwell on aversion, not be caught up in your reactions to their unpleasantness. Whether other people are pleasant or unpleasant, no matter what happens, you can choose your response.

According to the Doctrine of Mean (author unknown), "A person who is true to himself is a superior person. Because the superior person is true to himself (or herself), he is watchful over himself when he is alone. Self cultivation is primarily an internal process."

If you believe in this doctrine, you would like to live in peaceful co-existence, not creating problems for yourself or for others. You can't dwell in hatred or aversion because you hurt yourself, perhaps more than the person you do not like. With mindfulness, you recognise the aversion you feel, because you take care of what the pettiness of the mind is creating—you are conscious of the process. Social Psychology tells us that when we are critical of someone, we look for evidence or supposed evidence to support our assertions or assumptions. Our minds ignore the information which does not support our belief or proposition. If we are conscious, we will probably stop the circular thinking before finally labelling the person.

If we believe that a friend or a co-worker gossips about us or has betrayed us, it is not easy to forgive their behaviour. We may be tempted to dwell to an unhealthy extent on the injury we perceive they have done us. We may feel that we are letting ourselves down if we forgive others too easily. Some have even told me that if you ignore the insult or emotional hurt, the 'friend' will repeat the same behaviour again and again. However, if we do not forgive, we will be dwelling in aversion, which will reduce our peace of mind. Forgiving can lead to renewed friendship. Anger and hate use up energy that can best be utilised positively—for your own personal peace.

Many people will not agree with what I have said above. People see the faults in everything, but never look at themselves. People are focused on the outside, the faults are 'out there', but there is rarely any introspection. After self-analysis, if you feel that you are over critical of others, then it is time to get a handle on the way you interact with others. **Arrogance and self-awareness seldom go hand in hand**.

Please try these simple exercises:

If you are feeling aversion to somebody, meditate on it and think kindly of the person as a fellow human being who is facing difficulties and problems that arise in life just like you. Rather than dwelling in resentment, feel kindly towards the person and observe the aversion disappear.

Please answer the following questions if you believe that a friend has let you down or betrayed you:

- Have you talked to the friend or colleague and tried to understand their version of the story?

- Have you never criticised the friend or colleague behind their back?

- Was there an error in your assumptions or expectations?—correct it.

- Are there mistakes on both the sides?

- How can you correct the mistakes?

- What lessons have you learnt?

MIND AND BODY

Scientific interpretations of human beings inform us that we are a part of the physical order of nature. Human beings have size, shape, weight, and we are subject to physical and chemical laws. When we neglect the development of our health, of our body, we not only lose our health, but mentally we can lose our focus, our creativity, our courage and our peace of mind. On the other hand, attention to our body in the form of regular exercise increases our sense of self-control and self-mastery.

Having a healthy body leads to a healthy mind, reducing the risk of clinical depression and dementia in later life. Scientists at Bristol University in England found in December 2007 that physical exercise can reduce the risk of cognitive impairment or Alzheimer's in older people by between 30 and 40 per cent. There is strong evidence that exercise is vital for psychological well-being, mood and self-esteem. Physical activity prevents poor mental health, and in particular, depression. There are a number of reasons for the link, the main one being the release of chemicals in the brain that are associated with a positive mood. When we exercise, these chemicals are released. A recent educational study has shown that just five minutes of general jumping around at the start of the day results in improved concentration and improved learning. Any physical activity raises the heart rate and increases blood flow to areas throughout the body, including the brain.

As regards the mind, various studies have been written about the MIND. Some writers have not made any distinction between the brain and mind and have used them interchangeably in their works. I do not want to enter into the debate except to say that the Oxford dictionary defines mind as 'the seat of awareness, thought, volition, and feeling.' Another meaning given is: 'Attention, concentration (*my mind keeps wandering).'* Robert Winston in *The human **mind** and how to make the most of it,* says that "We *have* clearly arrived at a point where we understand something vital about the humankind: that the brain is the key organ responsible for what we are—that the 'mind' is created by the brain. We now know that there are regions in the brain that are responsible at least in part, for movement, sensation, and vision, and others even for such things as some religious experiences, and speech."

The mind and body continually interact in an infinite number of ways. Mind influences the body and body influences the mind. C.E.M. Joad in his book, *How our Minds Work,* explains the interaction thus: "If I am drunk, I see two lamp posts instead of one, if I fail to digest my supper, I have nightmares ... These are the instances of the influence of the body upon the mind. If I see a ghost, my hair will stand on end, if I am moved to anger, my face will become red, if I receive a sudden shock, I shall go pale. These are instances of the influence of the mind on the body."

So if we accept that the mind influences the body, then we need to be vigilant as to what the mind is up to, or be self-aware. Guru Nanak says that if the mind is impure, impure becomes the tongue and the body. The body is intimately connected with the mind.

In the same vein, if the body is sick, the mind also suffers. A pain in the stomach gives rise to melancholy. If the body is strong, then we have a healthy mind too. 'A healthy mind in a healthy body' is a truism that has been known to humankind for centuries. There is no doubt that if you want to keep your brain healthy, you should pay attention to your body.

Mrs Ackerman, an American science writer and author of *Sex, Sleep, Eat, Drink, Dream,* is an expert on what she calls "the drama unfolding inside"—during the 24 hours in the life of the typical human body. Her journey of discovery through the body's working has changed her life. She says, "I am more attuned to the importance of timing basic daily activities and I'm far more respectful of the body's needs, from regular exercise—which is good not only for the body but for brain—to frequent laughter (which boosts blood vessel health), enough natural light (to keep body in synchronicity with shifting seasonal cycles of light and dark), and especially adequate sleep.

"Most of us are getting too little sleep and sleep loss has a cumulative impact on our alertness, efficiency and thought processes. Sleep loss has a negative impact on our immune system, so you are more likely to get sick, it impairs the body's ability to process blood sugar and may lead to weight gain."

In December 2007, researchers from the University of Chicago Medical Centre reported a lack of sleep, especially deep or slow-wave sleep, reduces the body's ability to regulate blood sugar levels, increasing the risk of Type 2 diabetes, which is linked to obesity. Most experts on sleep recommend seven to eight hours sleep for adults and 9 to 10 hours for growing, energetic children.

As regards laughter, scientists think that when you hear a joke, a language centre on the left side of the brain makes sense of the words, and then sends the message over to the right side. There the frontal cortex delves into regions including those that store emotional and social memories, then shuffles the information until it clicks and you get the joke. Next, a structure deep in the brain pumps out dopamine—a "reward system" chemical that makes you feel good—and a primitive region near the base of your skull makes you laugh. Humour, it turns out, is a whole-brain experience with networks of brain parts—call them "humour muscles" passing signals to help us get a joke! According to years of psychological studies, many of which made the subjects laugh, humour can also loosen up our minds, allowing us to be more creative. So laugh and you will turbo-charge your brain!

Our body is smarter than we think, and it almost never lies. We can be more conscious of how our body's fluctuations—of temperature, stress hormones, blood pressure, heart rate, alertness, etc.—affect the way we function and feel. Mrs Ackerman says that "by listening to its signals, and paying attention to its rhythms, you can boost your health, your productivity and even your mood." We owe it to ourselves to know this better.

INTEELECT

According to the Oxford Dictionary, intellect is the faculty of reasoning, knowing and thinking, as distinct from feeling. The intellect is associated with cortical brain function. Cortex is the outer layer of the cerebrum, which is rich in neurons and in which 'thinking' occurs. Scientists say that it normally has a layer of neurons about 4mm thick.

Intellect is seldom applied to animals. It is believed that they do not have high levels of understanding or intelligence as humans. Humankind is superior to the rest of creation because of its character and intelligence, which have enabled it to bring great spheres of nature under its control. Elephants and horses may be big, but our ancestors trained them and brought them under their control. Oxen ploughed their fields and dogs guarded their houses.

Intellect is the part of the human mechanism which seeks to know the realities of the world and it determines and decides our position in the universe. It struggles for knowledge against difficulties. It goes deeper and deeper into things, understanding their meaning and exploring their nature and essence. Its function is to reason from the perception of the mind and the senses, to form conclusions and to put things into logical relations to one another. It is the intellect which discriminates between stone and diamond, between wheat and chaff, and discriminates what is good and what is bad, what is beneficial and what is harmful. This discrimination helps us to come to a final rational decision. People who run after a mirage come to realize later that they were chasing an illusion.

Intellect is also spirituality through which truth is realized. Intellect is a superior quality because it solves the various problems confronting humanity. Mind is controlled by intellect and in turn mind controls the senses. We need knowledge to develop the intellect and make the right choices. With the right choices we can evolve to the highest perfection or sink to the depths of degradation with the wrong decisions.

Read, understand and act on works by 'great thinkers' which give us the knowledge or the tools with which we can make the right choices. A little investment in the study of worthwhile works may be difficult initially, but it will yield results. Mere reading with no application is not of much benefit. Their real worth needs to be tapped. Science in the laboratory is of little use, unless taken advantage of or converted into technology.

If we underpin our intellect with the right knowledge, we will not make choices out of ignorance and then regret it or feel remorse and guilt. We will know what to choose, and it will be in accordance with our values and ideals. Just as water is contained by a pitcher, we need the 'right knowledge' to control the mind and train it.

MEDITATION—TO DEVELOP MINDFULNESS

Trivial and meaningless activities take most of our time and clog our minds. We find it difficult to concentrate on what is important because of the clutter in our minds. Cobwebs clog our minds because we are not mindful, we do not notice the working of the mind.

To practise mindfulness, sit in a comfortable position with your back straight. The small of the back should have its natural unforced curve. The ideal is an upright, alert posture with a straight spine, and the shoulders pushed back slightly so that they are not hunched.

Follow the sensation of your breath for some time as it follows through the nostrils and fills the chest and abdomen. Next, try maintaining your attention at one point—at the nostrils. Breath has a tranquillising quality, a relaxing quality, if it is not forced. Your mind will wander, but keep on retuning to the breath. Don't be put off by the mind wandering; be patient and persistent, and simply begin again—and again.

The aim is not to create a trance; the purpose here is to allow you to notice the working of the mind, the way it meanders into other things. We can even become engrossed in a train of thought, because it is natural for the mind to become absorbed in moods and thoughts. So instead of giving in to impatience, learn to let go and begin again. Move the attention to the breath in a gentle unforced way. Many people give up the practice too soon. Developing the ability to begin again and again leads to stability and ease.

The entire process involves gathering your attention, noticing the breath, noticing that the mind has wandered off, and to re-establish your attention. It develops mindfulness, patience and insightfulness.

DEPROGRAMMING THE MIND

> *"For many there is a kind of perverse pleasure in the self-righteous indignation one feels when one is treated unfairly."*

At a meeting of a charity, some people asked the stage secretary permission to address the audience. The stage secretary for some reason refused to share the platform with a member of what he perceived to be the 'opposition'. The 'opposition' grabbed the microphone after a small scuffle and said his piece. After that, whenever an attempt was made to reconcile or reach a compromise so that the charity should not suffer, the grieved person would invariably talk about the 'humiliation' he had suffered. Like a stuck record, the same story was repeated again and again. Some people choose to play the victim or the ultimate martyr and drown in self-pity.

There are some people who try to train their minds to cultivate spiritual values like compassion and tolerance at every opportunity. They practise these wonderful human qualities whenever there are conflicts with others or they are being treated badly by others.

A wise man was imprisoned with his disciples for many years. He was mistreated and abused in the prison. It was hard on the students when they saw their teacher being beaten and humiliated. They became very angry. But the teacher advised them not to be overcome by hatred, that this was an opportunity for inner development. He spoke to them about the importance of maintaining their compassion, even towards the guards who were sowing seeds for their future suffering by their misdeeds.

We form habits and then follow them slavishly. We all have friends who have sought our advice over the years and then carried on as before. They simply recreate and relive the same problems. In fact, they seem to seek them out. It is difficult to de-programme your mind from everything you have been doing, but if you are serious, then nothing is impossible. If you want to uncover the best in you, some incredibly strong parts have to be tempered, remoulded and redirected. You have to strike while the iron is hot, so to speak, or you tend to fall back into old habits or patterns, and rationalize why you do that. It may require deprogramming your mind from everything you have been doing to letting it be open, opening it up to be taught new techniques.

Let us see what others who managed to acquire an enduring sense of peacefulness have to say as quoted in *Quantum Leap*:

- "All this stuff I have been worrying about is unimportant. There is a whole new side of life to explore, to learn about."

- If I make less money, that's fine. I don't care. I just want to have a serene day-to-day life.

- What I get excited about now is walking in the woods, just taking in what is there, and celebrating the Creator.

RATIONAL BEINGS

People still debate whether human beings are rational or not, but philosophers have appealed to our rationality. Some people call it using 'common sense.' The emphasis on rationality was an important feature of Aristotle's teachings. A human being is part of the natural world, in that like the plants she ingests nutrients and reproduces herself, and like animals she moves around, perceives and has desires. But in addition and alone among all things, a human being is rational, and this is her defining mark or essence. One of the quirky things that make us human is that we can choose not to listen to our irrational desires. To be human is to reason, to employ sound or practical reason, in thinking how to live. An ideal life is lived in accordance with one's essence or deeply held values. It is a life of practical wisdom.

Unlike our animal friends, we all have a part in our brain called orbital frontal cortex that works like our executive officer. This voice can tell you to override the primitive part of the brain. Fine defines it thus: "A mere smudge of brain cells at birth, it takes twenty odd years or more to reach its full stature as the sergeant major of the adult brain. One of the many jobs of the prefrontal cortex is to regulate the emotional responses of less civilized brain regions, which is why it's a useful thing to have."

Rationality is what guides a person between, on the one hand, the over-indulgence of non-rational desires and on the other the suppression of them. For Socrates, 'rationality was self-mastery and the tireless search for truth.'

Sometimes it is a problem to explain how human beings are truly moral agents, that is, beings that act from free will, according to choices and decisions of their own. Some philosophers argue that we are determined and not determining. The problem of free will and determinism has remained one of the most intractable of difficulties. As this is not the remit of this book, I do not wish to dwell on the issue, but restrict myself to saying that unlike the animals, humankind is not tied to one kind of food.

Human beings can live on the hills or the plains and can make use of different resources and types of food that are available in a certain area. Man may not be as strong as the ox, but the ox draws his plough and a cow provides us with milk. Human beings talk, can accumulate knowledge, can remember the past and see into the future. We do not follow others like sheep, as we have the ability to know what is morally right and ethical and what is not. Through the combination of body and soul, human beings combine both the mortal world of time and matter with the eternal world of Spirit and Truth. We have the intelligence and potential to become anything we like. We have been endowed with the rationality and ability to take moral responsibility for our actions. Though we do not always think something through, wise people have a rational anticipation of what their actions and choices might result in.

Epictetus, the Greek Stoic philosopher, says, "The proper goal of our activity is to practise how to remove from one's life sorrows and laments and cries of 'alas' and 'poor me' and misfortune and disappointments." History tells us that Epictetus lived in Rome for many years as a slave, but eventually secured his freedom. Sometimes—no, to be more honest, quite regularly, we blame others for our misfortune and take credit for our achievements. Epictetus adds: "No one is a master of another's moral character and in this alone lays good and evil. No one therefore can secure the good for me, or involve me in an evil, but I alone have authority over myself in these matters." Contentment, peace of mind, and happiness are in your hands. Happiness is a state of your mind.

All this may appear to be commonsense, but the only problem with commonsense, remarked Voltaire, the French philosopher, is that it is not very common! Regrettably, it is an inestimable source of wisdom. It is I suppose for this reason that Epictetus used to ask his students, "How long will you delay to be wise?" You may wish to askyour self this question also.

No doubt the conditions of social life mean that an individual is subject to many constraints made necessary by the fact of living in the community with others. But still we have autonomy, and the autonomy in question is autonomy first and foremost of moral responsibility. Individuals have responsibility to make choices, rational choices, moral choices, about their life, and whatever the constraints, nobody can take that away from anyone.

THE MIND AND YOUR VALUES

The 'Mind' has been compared to a monkey by some thinkers. It flits from place to place and is restless even when sitting at one place. The mind is inconsistent—'It has a mind of its own.' It is your self-awareness, your intellect that can rein in the wayward mind and direct it to the goal. The intellect prevents the mind from wandering into different avenues.

Life is a play of opposites, success and failure, victory and defeat, loss and gain. A self-aware person draws strength from her disappointments and learns lessons from her successes so that they can be replicated. The secret of staying calm is to develop the internal balance that helps us to ride the ups and downs of life.

We are haunted by a sense of emptiness and incompleteness. In order to fill this emptiness, we try to acquire worldly goods. We chase one type of entertainment after another for fulfilment. Desires crop up in our minds all the time, and if a desire is not fulfilled, then the mind gets agitated, restless. When the mind is not at peace, we are unable to think clearly.

We are all seeking internal happiness and mental peace. It is right knowledge which can control our thoughts and our mind. If we are aware of our values that encompass what is important in our life and the welfare of the community at large also, then we have an aim in life, something to focus our mind and not concentrate on the trivia. The effort of achieving an ideal can offer profound meaning to life at every turn.

FOCUSING ON THE TASK IN HAND

We are all very busy with a myriad of tasks, concerns and projects at work and in daily life. We worry because it is difficult to focus on any one of them and almost impossible to focus on all of them. When we give our full attention to our worries, we become less effective in carrying out the tasks which we are expected to complete.

Many of us boast that we can do many tasks at the same time. Multi-tasking diminishes our ability to relax in certain situations. The brain copes much better with concentrating on individual tasks in sequence. Mrs Ackerman (expert on "drama folding inside") says, "I used to multi-task a lot, thinking I was getting more accomplished that way. No more. I realize now that it's safer, more efficient and more productive to do one thing at a time and devote my full attention to it." Keep it simple. We need a quiet mind to focus on the task at hand.

We can benefit from the practice of mindfulness—by blocking out everything except that which we need to stay focused on at any one time. Mindfulness is not easy, it has to be worked on, exercised to develop it and make it more effective. Once you have developed your mind, you can act with a clear mind, and be **present** now, i.e. focussed on the present and free of extraneous matters. Mindfulness frees us from mental obstacles. One does not pay much attention to the obstacles or automatic negative thoughts because the person is focused 'in the moment'. You are relaxed when you are focused. The focus comes with mindfulness. Your limiting beliefs cannot slow your progress to achieve your vision or improve a skill. Limiting beliefs are thoughts which tell you that you can't do this or achieve that.

- Don't think too much whether something you are keen on doing is possible, but concentrate on **how** it is possible.

PREJUDICES

Tyranny entrenches itself within the existing interest of the most refined citizens of a nation and says, 'If you dare trample upon these, be free.'

In the United Kingdom, we celebrated the bicentenary of the abolition of slavery on 25 March 2007. William Wilberforce was instrumental in abolishing slavery in the British Empire. In 1807 his bill for the abolition of slavery was passed and in 1833 largely through his efforts slavery was abolished partially in 1833 and completely in 1838 in the empire.

We need to ask ourselves whether we are really free too or are we bound by prejudice, cultural and social forces and inability to forgive. I went to Kenya when I was nine or ten years old. It was under British rule and everybody looked up to the white people. There was a social hierarchy whereby white people occupied the top positions, Asians were in the middle, and the Africans, the real inhabitants of the land were ranked third. The Africans were regarded as racially inferior. The education provided in the early part of the 20th century was basic, and designed to produce Africans who could work as clerks, court interpreters, and policemen within the colonial administration.

As a kid I absorbed the differentiation, even though it went against the tenets of my religion which advocates complete equality of human kind. It was only when I went to college that I started realizing that it was not right, that nobody was superior, and nobody was inferior. The social stratification was a social construct.

I studied Swahili which was the lingua franca of the country, and made a serious effort to acquaint myself with the local cultures. My respect for African people increased exponentially as I became aware of the richness of some of the tribal cultures and how much they had to teach us. I believe that we can be only free only if we are vigilant or mindful. Prejudice is normally based on ignorance; it is a pre-conceived opinion, a bias which may not have any foundation. Awareness of your prejudices will enable you to challenge them and accept others as equal.

SELF-AWARENESS

Cultivating self-awareness is a unique human endowment, but it is not easy. We all have blind spots, and we hold onto ideas and assumptions which serve no useful purpose.

We always judge others; make assumptions about others without even being aware of it. Quite often we act on our assumptions without checking whether they are facts, or if there is any evidence to support them. Self-awareness helps us to bring them into consciousness, and make them explicit. Once you are aware of them, you can think about them, and challenge them if necessary.

Self-awareness can lead to self-understanding, which is an act of comprehending one's actions and reactions. Self-awareness and self-understanding at a deeper level need to be grounded in reality. One needs to have an undistorted view of oneself, an accurate view of one's resources, abilities and limitations. The following story illustrates what can happen when we divorce reality and wallow in self-delusion:

A queen broke all the mirrors in her bedroom because they did not show her as beautiful. She called her servant and asked him to bring a mirror which would show her face in a more positive light. The servant brought a mirror and she broke it as soon as she saw her countenance in it. She reprimanded the servant for buying a poor quality mirror and gave him lot of money to buy a 'better mirror'. The servant brought another one, which she broke promptly as the looking glass reflected the image as it was—the reality. A mirror does not lie; it provides an accurate reflection.

The queen reprimanded the servant again and told him that if he did not bring her a mirror that showed her to be beautiful, she would break his face and bones as well. The servant was trembling as he went to the shops to buy a mirror which he knew did not exist and had not been manufactured. He met a sage who asked him the reason for his nervousness. The servant narrated the circumstances surrounding his dilemma and the wise man told him: "Get a mirror and once you have bought it, take me with you to the palace," The servant did as instructed and when they reached the palace, the queen was happy as she thought that the sage must have advised the servant how to buy a 'good' mirror.

She was about to break the looking glass again and lambaste the servant when the sage intervened and asked her to break her own face rather than the glass and the bones of the servant. He told her the truth that she was vain and her vanity stopped her from accepting the reality.

One cannot grow without self-understanding and self-knowledge. Only once you accept yourself as you are, warts and all, and are comfortable in your skin, can you develop or self-actualise. Self-actualisation was the term used by Abraham Maslow for the process whereby an individual comes to understand himself and thereby develop his talents and capacities with acceptance of his limitations. Self-awareness and self-understanding are basic requirements for the development of all aspects of your personality.

OBSTACLES TO ENHANCED SELF AWARENESS

To be self-aware is to be conscious of one's character, feelings and motives. The main ingredient of self-awareness is a greater grasp of reality. The main obstacles to self-awareness are arrogance or pride and low esteem. Arrogance arises when people have an inflated sense of their qualities and personal abilities. There are people who have pride in their might—which could be because of bravery or strength, wealth and power. Such people fail to realize that even great emperors have perished and been tuned to dust and ashes after their deaths. Some take pride in their beauty or attractiveness. They forget that the same Light shines in all the hearts and gives beauty. Beauty or attractiveness is very transient anyway; our youthfulness turns into old age sooner than we would like to acknowledge.

Then there are some who are arrogant because of their well-advertised charitable work. When virtuous deeds lead to pride and arrogance, then the higher aim is lost. Charity work should lead to humility and greater kindness as the benevolent person gets to understand the plight of the disadvantaged people.

An inflated sense of sense can be devastating as the individuals are constantly at odds with the world that refuses to see them as they see themselves, an unappreciated genius amongst people who have not evolved to the extent that they have. Those with an exaggerated sense of their accomplishment and talents blame others for their problems. They are perfect specimens on this earth, so others must be at fault. They fail to see how their actions affect others. A person consumed by false pride cannot be happy. It is a disease that must be overcome to attain inner sanity.

HOW TO OVERCOME THE OBSTACLES

- Accept one's arrogance and self-conceit just like an alcoholic needs to accept dependency on alcohol if therapy is to succeed.

- Identify the causes of the pride or arrogance. Is it money/wealth, power, status, etc.?

- Recognise their impermanence. Kings have become paupers and it is not uncommon for people from modest backgrounds to acquire wealth, status and power.

- Think of the areas you need to improve and take action. Set attainable goals.

PRAISE AND CRITICISM

It is not easy to retain your equanimity when you are criticised. We want to respond to the criticism in the strongest possible way. In the same vein, we are pleased and excited when we are praised. We like the individuals praising us and develop a close affinity with them. We swell like balloons when praised, but when the balloon bursts, there is agony. We are unhappy. We become attached to the praise, and it doesn't last very long. It is a temporary phenomenon, which the mind notices. We keep those individuals who are critical of us at a distance. Mindful people are fully aware of what is going through their minds; recognise their likes and dislikes, the things they are attracted to and their aversions. They are not overly happy when praised and dejected or unhappy when denigrated.

We can choose not to be affected by criticism, especially one that has no basis, or is not a fact, and retain our peace of mind. We do not have to hold on to either criticism or praise too tightly. You can recognise that you have a desire to be praised, and a dislike of being criticised. It was a wise person who said that 'we should be thankful to our enemies because they tell us about our weaknesses.' There can be no internal development, no real growth if we do not work on our weak points. Once you are conscious of how you allow external events to affect you, you are on the right path to maintaining your inner peace.

Having self-understanding which involves having a realistic view of one's abilities and limitations can help to cope with criticism confidently. With self-understanding you may not be able to control what the critic has to say, or the degree to which you are criticised, but you can choose not to be affected by it. If your personal self-assessment is grounded in reality, you will not be unduly affected by what other people have to say about your shortcomings or gaffes.

People are their own worst critics. That is why people who are their own strong critics are so hurt or angry when someone else criticises them. It is likely that a critic is saying what the person is already feeling or thinking.

If a criticism is valid, people with self-understanding will accept it in good faith and see it as an opportunity to advance their self-knowledge. On the other hand, if the criticism has no basis, they do not react strongly because they know it is not true. They may ask for evidence which supports the criticism and if none is produced, they know that it is not constructive feedback but destructive comments designed to undermine confidence. People with inner strength do not rely on other peoples' praise or lack of it, as they are aware of their capabilities and limitations. They know their successes, accomplishments and mistakes.

If a certain criticism hurts you strongly, you need to reflect why it affected you the way it did. Ask yourself:

1.   Are you afraid to be honest with yourself and acknowledge your limitations?

2.   What does the criticism teach you?

3.   How will you respond to a similar censure or comments in the future?

Useful Suggestions

- You can visualize yourself taking the criticism in your stride, and discussing the comments with the critic.

- Perhaps you need to affirm yourself. An affirmation could be:I am an open-minded person and will accept valid criticism to develop myself.

- Believe in the affirmation and behave like a person who accepts valid criticism for personal growth and development.

THE IDEAL SELF

Quite often we are not aware of 'Who we are' because we are too busy with our lives. It is only when one is aware of 'Who I Am' that one can think ahead of the

'Ideal self,' one's vision, a standard to aspire to or what one can be. For developing your ideal self or self-realisation, please ask yourself the following questions:

- What do I want to be or could be? What is my vision of my ideal self?

- How do I describe my real self now? What are my strengths and weaknesses?

- Which strengths of mine overlap with the Ideal Self?

- How do my real self and Ideal Self differ?

- What is my Learning Agenda to build on strengths while reducing gaps?

- Which new behaviours, thoughts and feelings do I need to experiment with?

- How will I practise the new behaviours so as to build new pathways and gain mastery over them?

- Who can encourage, support and help me in the process of self-realisation?

- Who will hinder me to realise my personal vision and master the new behaviours?

POWER OF CHOICE

When something disturbs our mind, we try to get away from it to escape. We do not want to think about or face difficult situations. We do not want to face certain issues, and we do not 'want to know certain people'. When running an 'Anger Management Course' or 'Keep Your Cool Group Programme' I often used to ask the participants: "What do you do when your partner is angry with you?" The answer quite often was: "I go out" or "I go to a pub." When we come back from the pub the issue has not dissipated; the conflict is not resolved but compounded.

Problems are not solved when you try to avoid facing them, but they do become more complicated. You may attain peace of mind for some time, but it will be short lived because you do not want to see things with your eyes and don't want to hear things with your ears. You can't bury your head in the sand for too long. We cannot be at peace because we are aware that there are external factors or stimuli which need our attention. If we don't pay heed to them, then we are going to have a very disturbing future.

When we decide not to run away from issues, but to face them with mindfulness, we realize that lack of equilibrium is not lost because of the issues confronting us, but because we allow them to affect us. We become victims of our circumstances. If you sit in a quiet place, relax your body and with a calm mind examine what effect the issue is having on you, notice your feelings—how sad, dejected, pleased, despondent you are. You will also become aware of how the mind becomes disturbed as a consequence of your feelings.

Once you know the things as they are, you can respond to them in a correct manner. Real tranquillity is born when we adopt the correct approach or the right response. You have the **Power of Choice, and you can choose it wisely.** You can choose how you want to be affected by whatever you have to meet. You take responsibility for the choices you make, and break free from the illusion that you are a victim of your circumstances. If we do not look at things as they are, we won't be at peace.

You can choose to see clearly as things are, not as imagined, and choose not to be affected by whatever you meet. Whatever others might be saying to you or doing to you does not affect you, because you choose that course of action. We do not have to follow the old ways; you can dramatically change your life! We can take stock of old ways, be aware of them, and keep cleaning them up.

It is worth noting that whatever our feelings may be, or our state of mind, they are not fixed, they are impermanent. We are happy one day and sad the other day, and quite often our moods change every few minutes. The state of the mind is not **yourself**, it is a temporary phenomenon. If you are mindful, you are aware of the conditions and not worried about them unduly, because you know that the sadness or ecstasy is impermanent.

We also need to be realistic and recognise that sometimes it is difficult to retain your equilibrium, and exercise your power of choice. At the time of writing this piece, I have got slight toothache. It is slight at this moment because the pain has been dulled by painkillers. I cannot concentrate when the pain become severe. The word 'somatic' pertains to the body and is supposed to be distinct from the mind. We cannot always separate the body and the mind. When the physical body is in pain, it does affect the mind up to a certain degree. But then some great souls have transcended their external conditions and said:

Stone walls do not prison a make,
Nor iron bars a cage,
Minds innocent and quiet take
That for an hermitage.

—'To Althea, from prison (1649)'

There are people like Mahatma Gandhi and Nelson Mandela who kept their dignity and inner peace while locked up in prisons.

DOING GOOD!

I have been active in a number of charities and find that people become too attached to their honorary positions. They join such bodies to serve, to do some good deeds, but gradually become attached to their positions. They do not want anybody else to take over. While doing 'service', they veer to the other side of the spectrum and lose their idealism. Their prime aim is abandoned, which was to serve regardless of any reward, to overcome their ego, but become pride ridden. Doing 'good' is supposed to bring good results, but then we do not know when to stop doing 'good' also. They serve so that they can be re-elected, which will boost their ego. I have seen such 'voluntary workers' come to blows at elections; they are scathing about the people who oppose them, and consider that they are the only ones who can carry out the tasks of the charity competently!

We get involved in anti-social activities because of our lust, pride, greed, uncontrolled anger and love of worldly possessions. Quite often we do good deeds because we want to boost our status, our ego, our standing in society, to become popular or for power, etc. Many religions very wisely state that suffering is caused by sins, and can be mitigated by performing good deeds. But, the factors which underpin our involvement in untoward activities can be virtually similar to those which form the basis of our 'charitable work.'

If people get involved in anti-social activities because of greed, etc., and pro-social activities to make a name for themselves, then the motives are not very different. Charity covers a multitude of sins. Philanthropic or charitable work is best when done out of love of human kind and not for self-aggrandisement. People in need should be helped, offered service, irrespective of their background, geographical area, colour or creed. Charity and altruism can bring a glow and happiness if given freely—without any ulterior motives.

Selfless service to others is good, it is a worthy ideal, but we can obtain optimal joy if our intentions and motivation are also right. It gives a meaning to our lives. So if you want real tranquillity, and happiness, please do help those in need, but be aware of your **motives** as well, otherwise you get rid of one type of chains i.e. of selfishness, and get chained to another type i.e. to inflated ego, fame, status, etc.

LIVING IN THE PRESENT

We should clearly understand that the past is gone, and the future has not yet arrived. If we think about it seriously, we realize that the present is the result of the past. The result of past actions is being experienced in the present. We reap the fruit of whatever we have sown. The future is still to come. Whatever does occur will be the result of our actions in the present. If we want a good future, we have to create it in the present by being fully aware of what we are doing now.

Once we start living in the present, we can dwell in peace, without anxiety about the past or worries about the future. We take other peoples' advice and try to learn about ways of attaining tranquillity, but our understanding is mostly intellectual. Mindfulness is something you have to work at, and only you can do it. Only you can fully know if you are mindful; only you can experience it through practice.

You may wish to ask yourself the following questions to ensure that you are living in the present:

- Do I dwell or reminisce too much about the past? If the answer is—Yes …

- How can I change it?

- Do I worry too much about the future? If the answer is—Yes …

- What am I doing now to create the future?

Conclusion

We all seek internal happiness and mental peace, but quite often in vain. We look for peace in idleness. We look for peace in quiet corners. We travel to distant places, go on pilgrimages but it still eludes us. But people who constantly accept themselves as they are, cultivate their self-awareness, and increase self knowledge, lead a spiritual life, progress further and gain internal strength. These components are all interconnected as:

- **Mindfulness**: Is the capacity to be fully aware of all that we experience inside us—body, mind heart and spirit, and what is happening around us. Mindfulness involves paying attention to thoughts, feelings and behaviours that are serving us well and those that are not. It also means to attend to the environment around us so that we can read the clues to see if things are going right or wrong.

- **Self Awareness**: It is closely aligned to Mindfulness as it is the ability to monitor our feelings, motives and our responses to enable us to deal more effectively with others.

- **Compassion**: Compassion helps us to be in tune with others, as it involves caring for them. Self compassion is a key to renewal and ignoring the 'victim syndrome.' What ever the moods, feelings, tensions, bodily tensions, with compassion to your self, you can be at ease with yourself. You can let go the negative emotions as you recognise their impermanent nature.

- **Reflection**: Reflection includes enquiry about our experiences and putting them into perspective. Self understanding or introspection involves having an insight about what we found through reflection and how it bears on our actions and reactions. It leads to self knowledge which is a comprehension of our motives etc.

Reflection is one way to build our path to renewal as it leads to transforming our ideas and future actions in the light of what we have learnt. We can meet the present moment with mindfulness, use reflection to resolve the problems and meet the next moment with purity of mind and courage. Without reflection, we can feel lost and find that inner peace eludes us.

- **Values**: Our values are reminders to bring back into consciousness what's really important in life to us. If we do not have any values, no **meaning in life**, we would forget ourselves and never seek to develop ourselves or seek inner peace. We will always look to outside things and people, the externals to keep us entertained.

- **Spirit**: At the deepest level, we all want to know, "Who AM I?" and have some 'intrinsic awareness' of our spirituality. The spirit or the small voice inside serves you best when you set your mind aside. We do not want to be bound by the mind with its fears and doubts but learn to trust the spirit. The 'inner voice' can guide us to develop a philosophy of life based on ethical principles and the high values.

We are ignorant of the tremendous potential that lies within us and spend our life chasing trivialities. Sometimes we say to our self,"I am an ordinary person, can I realize my full potential?" We set imaginary limitations and never open our eyes to larger possibilities. We need to delve into our personalities and uncover the greatness within.

If you are aware of your values, that is, the higher values, it is very likely that they will be sacred to you. You will pursue them with passion, your full energy and dynamism. You have to taste the food, eat and then digest it to attain the full benefit. If you throw it up, it will not supply you with the energy—the proteins and the carbohydrates and the vitamins you need to perform efficiently. Similarly, we have to live by our values, act on them and not only talk about them.

One can only derive full satisfaction if one is focused on the higher aims which give meaning to life—fulfil the purpose of life. Focus means the ability to say 'NO' to anything which we do not wish to get involved in. Human beings are permeable and we are affected by the turmoil around us. Without ceasing to love those around you, or serving others, detach yourself a little to renew yourself. Our first task is to preserve our own sanity or we are no use to anyone. Focus on yourself, your sanity, your inner self, and look at the needs of the body, heart and spirit and how you can develop your intellect to satisfy them. Our thoughts can be very powerful. If focused, they are a force to reckon with.

With inner strength, and self awareness, one is able to confront the emotions and personal demons which arise and gradually they loosen their hold over the person. With responsible choices, people can change their behaviour and cultivate a healthy personality. There is no accumulation of inner strength without making choices that stretch us. You can use your inner strength to transform your life. With the right choices, you can evolve to the highest perfection.

There will be challenges of course. The process will not be quick. It will be uneven, punctuated by setbacks and achievements. It will require considerable resolve and continuous commitment. But we are sentient beings, who have the freedom to choose, and not to remain in a prison of our own making. If we are resolute, we can overcome our past and obtain release from the self imposed prison. Our higher values are our building blocks; we can use them to ascend to where ever we want to be, to make our life meaningful.

When we make choices that are in line with our mission in our life, our soul and heart, we become alive, creativity flows, and all that is done, all the tasks undertaken have a meaning. When we observe fulfilment in our life, and in the lives of others, we know that our life has a purpose, a meaning and we live it.

Living according to your values, your mission in life is a process, not an event. When you know about where you want to be, your direction in life is crystal clear, your journey is chalked out, your thoughts remain focused on the spiritual path, and not on pandering to your selfish desires. Your attitude to your ideals, your commitment and sacrifice to your higher values, add completely a new dimension, a meaning to an otherwise routine life. You will do what it takes to live with your values. You experience peace when you dedicate or consecrate your actions to the Goal. You are resolute and withstand forces that take you away from your higher aims. The higher the goal to which you surrender, the more your inner strength develops. You will be living a spiritually enriched life, at peace with yourself and at peace with the world. Inner peace and spiritual growth go hand in hand. It is a win—win situation.

Tansen was a famous musician in Akbar, the mogul emperor's court. One day, Akbar expressed a wish to hear Haridas, Tansen's teacher sing. This was arranged and when he heard Haridas sing, the emperor was stunned as he had never heard a melody sung so sweetly before. Akbar then asked Tansen to sing the same song which his teacher had sung. After hearing Tansen sing, Akbar said there is a difference between Haridas's rendering of the melody and yours. What is it? Tansen replied,"I sing to please you, he sings to please the Higher Being".

This book may clarify your mind, it has done the talk, but you will have to walk to find out whom you want to please in quest of your own inner peace.

Good Luck

Appendix

If you have read the whole book, I assume that you have also done some of the exercises aimed at helping you to grow and develop mentally spiritually emotionally and intellectually. It is possible that you have practised and pursued some of the values which are most important to you. You are more conscious of what values and habits serve you and which do not. I believe that you have discovered which values assist you to find meaning and purpose in life, and the ones that support you in your quest for inner peace.

You may recall that in the in the Chapter on Values, you were asked to select ten values which are most important to you. You were also asked to retain the rankings so that you can repeat the same exercise again to find if there is any change in your values. It is possible that what was important to you three or four months ago, has lost its significance. The same exercise repeated below will assist you to become conscious as to what is really important to you now and then embody it.

YOUR VALUES (What is most important)

Following are some Values in an alphabetical order. From the list, identify the top ten which are most important to you. Place 1 (one) next to the value which is most important and 2 next to the value which is second most important, and so on.

1. Acceptance—to be accepted as I am

2. Ambitious—hard working, aspiring

3. Broadminded—tolerant, open minded

4. Capable—competent, effective

5. Caring—kind, humane

6. Comfortable life—to have a pleasant enjoyable life

7. Contribution—to give money or help to a common cause

8. Compassionate—merciful, willing to alleviate suffering.

9.   Courageous—standing up for your rights

10. Ecological—to live in harmony with the environment

11. Faithful—logical, trustworthy

12. Famous—well known, socially recognised.

13. God's will—to seek and obey God's will

14. Growth—to keep changing and growing

15. Happiness—contentedness

16. Healthy—to be physically well

17. Helpful—giving help, being useful

18. Honest—sincere, truthful

19. Independent—self reliant, free from dependency

20. Inner peace—personal peace

21. Intellectual—intelligent, reflective

22. Logical—rational

23. Loving—affectionate

24. Moral—concerned with the distinction between right and wrong

25. Obedient—dutiful

26. Power—to have control over others

27. Responsible—dependable, reliable

28. Self-controlled—self-disciplined

29. Service—to be of service to others

30. Tolerance—to accept and respect those different from me

31. Virtue—to live a morally pure life

32. Wealth—Plenty of money

33. Wisdom—to have a mature understanding of life

After you have ranked the values and prioritized the **TEN** most important to you, please answer the following questions:

1. How do you feel about the way you have ranked the values? (on a scale of 1 to 10 write the number which describes how you feel—10 signifies that you do care much about the order in which you ranked the values, and 1 (one) tells you that you do not care much about the order in which you ranked the values. Or—Do you feel that your ranking was a bit haphazard and you did not give it much thought. Did you do the ranking conscientiously?

2. How satisfied do you feel about the way you have ranked the values?

3. Which rankings do you feel satisfied or dissatisfied with?

4. Do you find the exercise thought provoking?

5. Do you think it will lead you to do some more thinking about your values?

6. How would a person who really values personal peace, and retains equanimity what ever the circumstances rank the same values?

References

1. Bowker, J. (ed.) (2002), *The Oxford Dictionary of World Religions,* Oxford, BCA.

2. Bowlby,J., *Attachment and Loss,*(1998), Pimblico

3. Boyatiz, R. McKee, A. (2005), *Resonant Leadership,* Boston, Harvard Business School.

4. Claxton., Lucas, B., (2004), *Be Creative: Essential Steps to Revitalize Your Work and Life*, BBC Worldwide Press Release

5. Cross, R., (ed.) (1994), *Swimming Teaching and Coaching*, ASA Swimming Enterprise Ltd.

6. Covey, S. R. (2004), *The Seven Habits of Highly Effective People,* London, Simon and Schuster.

7. Fine, C., (2006), *A Mind of its Own: How your brain distorts and deceives,* Cambridge, Icon Books Ltd.

8. Frankl, V.E., (2000), *Man's Search for Ultimate Meaning,* New York, Basic Books.

9. Goleman, D. 1998), *Working with Emotional Intelligence,* London, Bloomsbury.

10. Grayling, A.C., (2004), *The Search for the Best Way to Live*, Weidenfield and Nicholson.

11. Higaona M.,(1985), *Traditional Karate-do Vol.1,* Tokyo, Minato Research and Publishers,

12. HH Dalai Lama, Cutler, H., (2003), *The Art of Happiness at Work,* London, Hodder and Stoughton.

13. James, O. (2007), *Affluenza*, Vermillion

14. Lynch, J. *Creative Coaching*, (2000), Human Kinetics.

15. McGreal,I.P.(ed.) (1995) *Great Thinkers of the Eastern World: The major thinkers and the philosophical and religious classics of China, India, Japan, Korea, and the world of Islam*, New York, Harper Collins publishers.

16. Miller, R.W., C'De Baca. (2001), *Quantum Change: When Epiphanies and Sudden Insights Transform Ordinary Lives*, New York, The Guildford press

17. Muller, C., (2000), *Have Anything You Really Really Want: A Christian Testimony*, Lincoln: Writers Club Press.

18. Porter, K. (2003), *The Mental Athlete*, Human Kinetics

19. Rokeach, M. (1973). *The Nature of Human Values*, Free Press

20. Row, J. (2007), *The Complete Power*, Mumbai, Vedanta Vision.

21. Row, J. (2007), *Profile of the Perfect Person*, Mumbai, Jaico Publishing House.

22. Sikka, A.S. (1979), *Philosophy of Mind in the Poetry of Guru Nanak*, Ludhiana, Sikka Publishing House.

23. Singh, S. (2007), *Achieving a Healthy Balanced Life!*, iUniverse, Inc.

24. Sumedho, A. (1992) *The Four Noble Truths*, Hertfordshire, Amravati Publications.

25. Sumedho, A (2004), *Intuitive Awareness*, Hertfordshire, Amravati Publications.

26. Winston, R. (2003), *The human mind and how to make the most of it*, London, bantam Press.

27. Zukav, G. Francis, L. (2004), *The Mind of the Soul: Responsible Choices*, Simon and Schuster,

Index

978-0-595-50493-0
0-595-50493-0

Printed in the United Kingdom
by Lightning Source UK Ltd.
130249UK00001B/151/P